NORTH CAROLINA

NORTH CAROLINA BY ROAD

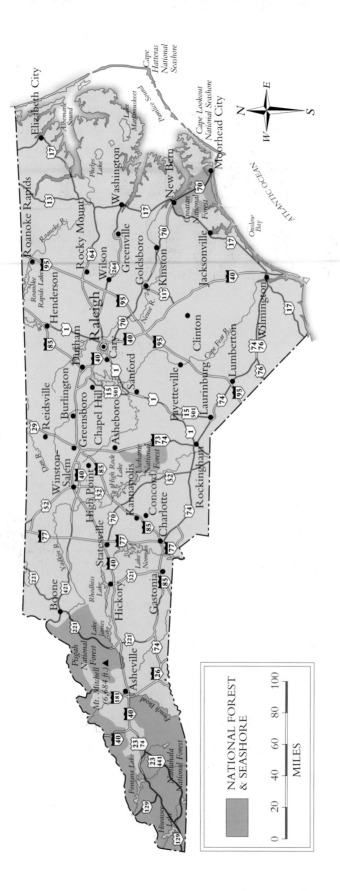

NATIONAL FOREST
& SEASHORE

MILES

0   20   40   60   80   100

CELEBRATE THE STATES
NORTH CAROLINA

David Shirley

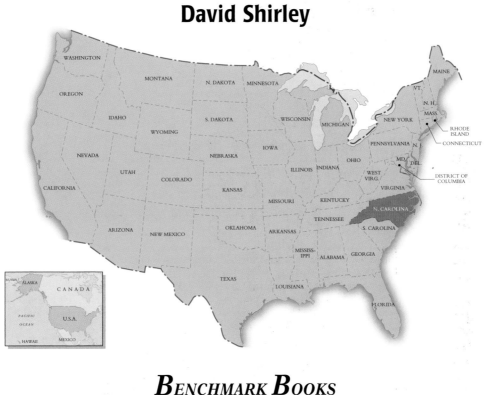

BENCHMARK BOOKS

MARSHALL CAVENDISH
NEW YORK

Benchmark Books
Marshall Cavendish Corporation
99 White Plains Road
Tarrytown, New York 10591-9001

Library of Congress Cataloging-in-Publication Data

Shirley, David, (date)
North Carolina / David Shirley.
p.   cm. — (Celebrate the states)
Includes bibliographical references (p.) and index.
ISBN 0-7614-1072-4 (lib. bdg.)
1. North Carolina—Juvenile literature. [1. North Carolina.]
I. Title. II. Series
F254.3 .S55 2001   975.6—dc21   00-031847

Maps and graphics supplied by Oxford Cartographers, Oxford, England

Photo Research by Candlepants Incorporated

Cover Photo: Corbis/Gary W. Carter

The photographs in this book are used by permission and through the courtesy of: *Corbis*: Franz-Marc Frei, 6-7; William Blake, 10-11; David Muench, 15, 19, 112; Phillip Gould, 17, 98-99; Patrick Johns, 23; Joe McDonald, 24; Layne Kennedy, 25; Jim Zuckerman, 26 (top), Annie Griffiths Belt, 26 (lower),72; Bob Rowan, 28; Mariners Museum, 33; Bettmann,47, 52-53, 87, 96, 126, 127, 131, 132, 133 (lower); Owen Franklin, 57, 84-85, 101; Jacques M. Chernet, 58; Kevin Flemming, 60, 74, 114-115; Raymond Gehman, 62, 80, 102, 136; H. David Seawells, 63 (right); Farrewll Grehan, 63 (left); James L. Amos, 68-69; Daniel Laine, 89; Mosaic Images, 92, 133 (top); Mitchell Gerber, 95; Buddy Myes,105; Jim McDonald, 107; Carl Corey, 124; Henry Diltz, 128; John Garrett, 129; AFP, 130; Corcoran Gallery of Art, 134; Tim Wright, back cover. *Photo Researchers Inc.*: Robert Alexander, 21; Stephen J. Kraseman, 117 (right); George Ranali, 117 (left); Jany Sauvanet, 121. *North Carolina Museum of Art, Raleigh, Gift of Mr. and Mrs. George D. Finch*, 30-31. *North Carolina Collection, University of North Carolina library at Chapel Hill*: 35, 44, 46,. North Carolina Museum of History: 38. *Woolaroc Museum, Bartlesville OK*: 42. *North Carolina State Archives*: 49, 90. *Transparencies Inc.*: Kelly Culpepper ,66; Jane Faircloth, 71, 104, 111; *North Carolina Travel and Tourism*; 77, 78, 125.

Printed in Italy

3   5   6   4   2

CONTENTS

NORTH CAROLINA IS . . .

North Carolina is a land of pure white beaches . . .

"The most beautiful sight I've ever seen is at the beach at Nags Head. I can just see the foamy blues waves of the Atlantic Ocean lapping up against the white sand. You can crawl up atop the dunes and watch as sheets of sunlight dance across the water and see the strong waves drag the sand back into sea." —a Wake Forest resident

. . . and dramatic mountain views.

"Sometimes I'll be hiking along one of the trails, with the trees so high and thick that I can barely see my way. And then I'll stumble unexpectedly upon a clearing in the trees and suddenly see those deep, blue layers of mountains spreading out in every direction. After all these years, it still leaves me speechless. I honestly believe that standing there, in the middle of those great mountains, is as close to heaven as you can get." —resident of Boone

North Carolina is the home of the old and the new.

"We've always had the strangest mix of people. I mean, on one hand, we've got some of the most liberal people and institutions in the nation. There's the proud Quaker tradition and the whole history of religious liberalism. And, of course, there's all the groundbreaking research that takes place at Duke University, the University of North Carolina, and the Research Triangle. But at the same time, you have to remember that this is the same state that keeps electing Jesse Helms—the most conservative person in the

Senate—year after year. I guess we just like to disagree."

—a government employee in Raleigh

It is a place to dream about . . .

In my mind, I'm going to Carolina.
Can't you feel the sunshine.
Can't you just see the moonshine.
Maybe just like a friend of mine
It hit me from behind.
And I'm going to Carolina in my mind.

—from "Carolina in My Mind," by James Taylor

. . . and a place to live.

"Lord, it's just like living in a poem.
I like calling North Carolina home."

—North Carolina State Board of Travel and Tourism

North Carolina is all this and more. A land of physical extremes, it has immense mountain peaks, gentle rolling meadows, and broad, sandy beaches. It is a place where people disagree over the value of tradition and the promise of change. In spite of their differences, North Carolinians share a competitive spirit in all areas of life—from sports to music to politics. From the mountains to the beaches, from the city to the countryside, North Carolinians are working together to improve their state and the quality of their lives together.

1 THE BLUEST SKIES IN THE WORLD

From the sandy, white coastline of the Atlantic Ocean to the towering peaks of the Appalachian Mountains, North Carolina is full of natural wonders and breathtaking beauty. "You don't have to go very far to find something beautiful or amazing in this state," says a college instructor from Durham. "We've got the prettiest beaches on the East Coast, the highest mountains east of the Mississippi River, and the bluest skies you'll find anywhere in the world. I just don't think you can find a more beautiful place to visit—or to live."

Despite its variety, North Carolina is not large. It ranks twenty-ninth in size among the fifty states. To the east, the Atlantic Ocean forms North Carolina's entire state line. Tennessee forms its boundary to the west. To the south are South Carolina and Georgia, while Virginia is to the north.

THREE REGIONS

North Carolina is divided into three regions: the Atlantic Coastal Plain, the Piedmont Plateau, and the Appalachian Mountains.

The Atlantic Coastal Plain. The coastal plain includes both the narrow, sandy shores of the Atlantic and the broad plains and pine forests that spread nearly one hundred miles west toward the center of the state. Throughout the summer, the flat fields of the

LAND AND WATER

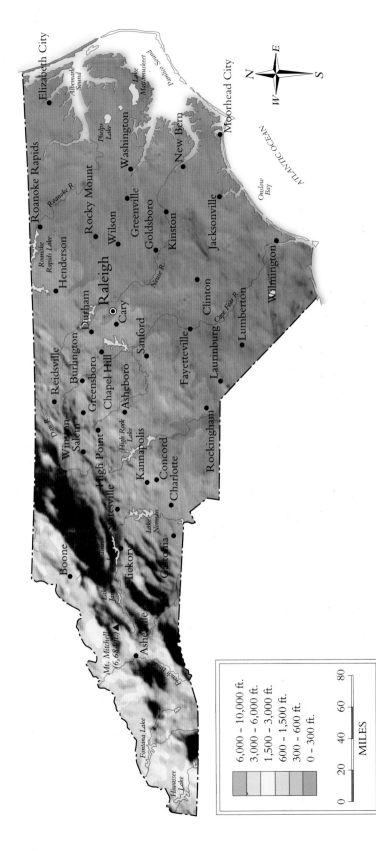

Elizabeth City

Albemarle Sound

Lake Mattamuskeet

Pamlico Sound

Moorhead City

N
E
W
S

Roanoke Rapids

Roanoke R.

Phelps Lake

Washington

New Bern

ATLANTIC OCEAN

Roanoke Rapids Lake

Rocky Mount

Wilson

Greenville

Goldsboro

Kinston

Jacksonville

Onslow Bay

Henderson

Raleigh

Neuse R.

Wilmington

Roanoke R.

Durham

Cary

Sanford

Clinton

Reidsville

Burlington

Chapel Hill

Asheboro

Fayetteville

Laurinburg

Lumberton

Cape Fear R.

Greensboro

Dan R.

Winston-Salem

High Point

High Rock Lake

Kannapolis

Concord

Rockingham

Statesville

Charlotte

Boone

Lake James

Lookout

Hickory

Lake Norman

Gastonia

Asheville

Mt. Mitchell (6,684 ft.) ▲

French Broad

Fontana Lake

Hiwassee Lake

6,000 – 10,000 ft.
3,000 – 6,000 ft.
1,500 – 3,000 ft.
600 – 1,500 ft.
300 – 600 ft.
0 – 300 ft.

0   20   40   60   80

MILES

coastal plain are filled with peanuts, soybeans, sweet potatoes, and tobacco. Farther east toward the Atlantic Ocean, the region's many rivers, streams, and bays spill out across the rich farmland to form sprawling swamps and muddy marshlands. Here and there, the thick trunks of live oak trees and bald cypress rise proudly out of the watery landscape.

At the state's northeast corner is the enormous Dismal Swamp. "It truly is a lonely, dismal sight," explains a Creswell resident. "I think it has something to do with the way the heavy clouds settle down over the dark waters at sunset. And the way the thick brush just gets deeper and denser the further you look. I bet I've been here a hundred times, and the place still gives me the creeps. But in spite of that, there's an element of mystery to the place, something that makes you want to wander in and take your chances."

To this day, most of the Dismal Swamp remains unsettled and undeveloped. The area's muddy soil is covered with dense thickets of wild grapes, swamp blackberries, green briers, and trumpet vines. Poisonous snakes—such as water moccasins, copperheads, and canebrake rattlesnakes—make their homes beneath the undergrowth. Although a number of roads and bike paths have been cut through the junglelike terrain in recent years, it is still almost impossible to explore the area on foot. Locals say the Dismal Swamp is full of the bodies of hunters and hikers who wandered into the dense marshland—but never returned.

Most of North Carolina's coastline is protected from the strong winds and rough waters of the Atlantic Ocean by a string of sandy reefs and narrow islands. Known as the Outer Banks, this chain of islands stretches all the way from the state's northern border to

Even today, it is hard to get through the Dismal Swamp. "I suspect the first settlers in the area must have seen it as the absolute end of the road," says one North Carolinian.

Cape Lookout in the south. The Outer Banks is prized for its pure, sandy beaches that run like a brilliant white ribbon between the mainland and the Atlantic's deep blue waters. At Nags Head and Kill Devil Hills, the flat beaches rise up dramatically into high sand dunes. The highest of these dunes have colorful names, like Graveyard Hill, Scraggly Oak Hill, and Jockey's Ridge, and offer

THE LADY OF THE LAKE

The Dismal Swamp is filled with a strange plant called foxfire, which absorbs sunlight during the day and emits an eerie green glow at night. Over the years, many legends have arisen as locals have mistaken the glow of foxfire for fantastic creatures from ghosts to flying saucers. Here's one.

Long ago, a young Indian maiden died a few days before her wedding day. After her death, the warrior who was to have married her became deeply depressed. He refused to talk to anyone and spent more and more time sitting and walking by himself.

One dark evening, the young warrior told his friends that he had seen his lost love paddling a white canoe across the waters of a nearby lake. The young man became obsessed with the idea that the maiden had left her grave and paddled into the darkness of the Dismal Swamp. Each night, he walked to the edge of the swamp and waited, as if he expected her to show up. Finally, he left his village for good. His friends believed that he had gone into the swamp in search of her. He was never heard from again.

magnificent views of the ocean to anyone willing to climb them. "I love the beaches here in the fall, after all the other tourists have gone back home," explains a man with a beach house near Nags Head. "You can walk for hours and never see another person. There's nothing but the wind and the waves and the seagulls and terns flying overhead. It's absolutely breathtaking."

The Appalachian Mountains. The Appalachian region, which forms the western border of the state, is composed of many

A beach along the Outer Banks is the perfect place to admire the deep blue Atlantic Ocean.

connecting mountain ranges, including the Blue Ridge Mountains and the Great Smoky Mountains. All are part of the Appalachian Mountains, which stretch from Georgia to Maine. The region is famed for its spectacular colors, which come from the wide variety of trees—more than 120—that thrive there. In fact, the mountains of North Carolina are home to more types of trees than exist in all the countries of Europe combined. The area is the most beautiful in the early morning or just before sunset, when clouds of fog often settle like a smoky blue haze over the dark mountains. The Cherokee Indians who lived in the area before the first European settlers arrived referred to the North Carolina mountains as "the place of blue smoke."

Among the most spectacular sites in the region are the towering peaks of Grandfather Mountain and Mount Mitchell, which at 6,684 feet is the highest point in North America east of the Black Hills of South Dakota. Rising far above the clouds, these majestic peaks provide visitors with panoramic views of the mountains stretching north and west.

The Piedmont Plateau. The region of soft, rolling hills in the center of the state is called the Piedmont Plateau. Although its countryside is clustered with farms, it is known primarily for its industry and sprawling cities. The five largest cities in the state—Charlotte, Greensboro, Winston-Salem, Durham, and the capital city of Raleigh—are all in the Piedmont.

In the Piedmont's southeast corner are the Sandhills. In contrast to the heavily urban northern and western Piedmont, the Sandhills are mostly rural. Here, grassy hills, peach orchards, and pine forests are much more common than the occasional small town. With its vast green meadows, the Sandhills are a popular spot to raise horses. You can often see the magnificent creatures grazing and running freely along the hillsides.

RIVERS AND WATERFALLS

In addition to its long coastline, North Carolina has abundant

The mountains of western North Carolina are famous for their peaceful waterfalls.

rivers, streams, and waterfalls. Mountainous western North Carolina is filled with cascading waterfalls, crystal lakes, and cool running streams. In all, the state boasts more than three hundred waterfalls, including Whitewater Falls, the highest waterfall on the East Coast at 411 feet. Most of the state's waterfalls are hidden away deep in the forests. Hikers can often hear the steady stream of water splashing onto the rocks long before they can see it.

The state is also crisscrossed by rivers. The New River is narrow, deep, and rapid. Most of the state's rivers, however, are wide and peaceful. Broad rivers like the Cape Fear and the Neuse provide seagoing vessels with easy access to inland ports.

North Carolina's most spectacular waterway was actually made by human beings. For most of the state's history, harsh winds and rough waters were a constant danger for ships sailing from one end of the North Carolina coast to the other. The Intracoastal Waterway was constructed during the early twentieth century to provide sailors with a safe passage over calm waters. It connects the natural inland waterway between the Outer Banks and the mainland with dozens of rivers, streams, and small lakes along the coast, forming one continuous inland canal. Each year, the waterway provides smooth sailing for thousands of barges and boats making their way up and down the coast.

TREES AND PLANTS

Along with the dramatic diversity of its terrain, North Carolina provides sightseers with a stunning variety of trees, flowers and other plants.

The dense mix of red spruce, Fraser fir, hemlock, and tulip poplars that crowd the mountains' lower slopes give them a deep, blue-green hue. All along the mountainsides, purple mountain laurel, orange flame azalea, and pink catawba rhododendron provide splashes of color.

Dazzling yellow blooms sprout on these towering tulip poplars each spring.

The hillsides of the Piedmont are filled with huge oak and hickory trees, which tower above the red maple trees, dogwoods, and sourwoods that crowd the lowlands. To the south, the wooded areas of the Sandhills are dominated by longleaf pines. Throughout the Piedmont grow an astonishing variety of wildflowers, often in dazzling, multicolored combinations. Among the more common are the brilliant orange blossoms of the daylily, the tiny purple buds of the blazing star, and the full red petals of the Shirley poppy.

The warm, damp weather and sandy shores of the coastal plain and barrier islands create an ideal environment for oaks, loblolly pines, and cabbage palms. The coastal plain is also full of insect-eating plants, such as the Venus flytrap and the pitcher plant. The sweet, syrupy liquid that coats the inside of the pitcher plant's deep, funnel-shaped leaf attracts wasps and bees. Once inside, the insect is trapped by the sticky nectar and slides down the full length of the pitcher, where it drowns in a pool of nectar.

ANIMAL LIFE

Animal life also varies widely from one end of the state to the other. The dense mountain forests of western North Carolina are home to beavers, bobcats, boars, and black bears. Mountain hawks soar high above the trees. The North Carolina mountains are also an ideal place to find salamanders. In fact, more species of salamander live in the region than anywhere else in North America. The giant spotted salamander known as the hellbender can easily be sighted scurrying near the entrances of caves or resting on shaded, moss-covered stones.

The pitcher plant is one of North Carolina's strange insect-eating plants. Bugs are lured inside by its nectar and then they can't get out again.

Many woodpeckers and hawks nest in the Piedmont's woods. The area's meadows and farmlands are filled with bobwhite quails and cardinals, North Carolina's state bird. Wild turkeys, white-tailed deer, raccoons, fox squirrels, and scarlet king snakes are also common in the region.

The Piedmont's many wildflowers attract a colorful array of but-

The brightly colored scarlet king snake is common in North Carolina.

terflies. On summer afternoons bright butterflies such as the painted lady and the tiger swallowtail flit lazily from flower to flower. And
on summer evenings, street lamps attract an astonishing assortment
of gigantic moths, including the deep green pandora sphinx and the
yellow-and-orange imperial moth. The most breathtaking of these
enormous insects is the rare pale green luna moth, which can sometimes be seen along the state's roadsides and forest paths.

The coastal plain and barrier islands provide a natural refuge for
an incredible variety of birds. More than four hundred species live
along the Outer Banks alone, with another one thousand species
migrating along the coastline each spring and fall. Ospreys, terns,

THE RED WOLF

The shy red wolf is one of the scarcest species in North Carolina. With its reddish brown fur and black streaks, it is also one of the most attractive.

The red wolf originally lived in the southeastern United States. By the 1960s, however, hunting and land development had driven the wolves from their homes. Fortunately, scientists were able to keep a few of the animals alive in captivity until they could find some-place for them to live.

The red wolf was reintroduced to North Carolina in 1987. At that time, several were released into the marshland around Alligator River. The area was chosen for its warm weather and the absence of hunters and land development. The area was also ideal because the white-tailed deer, raccoons, and other small animals that live there provide the wolves with abundant prey.

After the wolves were released, they quickly began to reproduce. As soon as a newly born red wolf is located, it is outfitted with a radio transmitter. This enables scientists to keep track of its where-abouts and safety. So far, the project has been extremely successful. Today, only 145 red wolves are known to exist in the wild. Of these, 83 live among the forests and marshlands around Alligator River.

Butterflies, including the tiger swallowtail, abound in the Piedmont.

Pelicans are one of the many creatures that attract bird lovers to the Outer Banks.

pelicans, and barn owls are among the more common birds found in the area. The ocean waters off the North Carolina shore are filled with life, including loggerhead turtles, humpback whales, dolphins, and such tropical fish as the mahi-mahi and the wahoo.

PERFECT WEATHER

With its long, mild summers and clear blue skies, North Carolina is a popular destination for tourists in search of warm beaches, calm mountain lakes, and all types of outdoor recreation. The average high temperature is ninety degrees during July and August. The average low temperature during December and January varies from twenty-eight degrees in Asheville in the mountains to forty degrees in Wilmington on the coast.

North Carolina receives a generous amount of rain and snow during the year. The southwestern hills receive seventy-five inches a year, while the northwestern mountains get forty inches. Across the state, the heaviest rain occurs during the hot days of July and August. Average snowfall varies dramatically from one region to another, with up to thirty inches accumulating in the mountains and usually less than two inches along the shore.

In spite of its generally pleasant conditions, North Carolina's weather can occasionally be extreme. Most of the time, the Outer Banks protects the rest of the state from the powerful storms that strike between June and November. In the late 1990s, violent weather struck the shore with even greater force than usual. Several major storms blew across the barrier islands and onto the mainland. One of the most destructive was Hurricane Fran, which pounded the area around Cape Fear with 115-mile-per-hour winds in 1996. By the time the storm lifted, it had caused more than $1 billion in damage.

But North Carolina is best known for the calm weather that follows the storms and the crystal blues skies that provide the backdrop for the state's stunning landscapes. Although there is no scientific evidence to support their claims, many North Carolinians say that, on clear days, their state has the bluest skies in the world.

To many people, North Carolina is heaven on earth.

"You can laugh if you want to," says a contractor from Elizabeth City, "but we really do believe that the sky is bluer here than anywhere else. Maybe it's just the way the sky looks against the white beaches and those dark leaves up in the mountains. I don't know. But you can travel anywhere you want—and, believe me, I've been to a lot of places in my life. But when you come back home to North Carolina, you'll swear this state has the bluest skies and the most beautiful scenery of anywhere you've ever been."

2 PROTEST AND PROSPERITY

Falls at Tamahaka, by William Frerichs

Throughout its history, North Carolina has been prosperous. In its earliest years, the region's abundant natural resources made North Carolina an attractive place to settle. More recently, the inventiveness and hard work of North Carolinians have helped the state continue to thrive. But great sacrifices and protests have sometimes been required to bring prosperity and freedom to all the state's citizens.

NATIVE AMERICAN LIFE

In the days before Europeans first sailed into the region, North Carolina was home to about thirty Native American groups, including the Tuscaroras, the Hatteras, the Catawbas, and the Cherokees.

The Tuscaroras and the Hatteras were among the tribes that lived in small villages near the ocean or along rivers and streams. Villagers often built walls or dug ditches around their settlements to protect themselves from enemies and predators. They got food by farming, fishing, and hunting with bows and arrows.

The Cherokees lived in small villages in the Appalachian Mountains in western North Carolina. They cut trees to build homes and canoes and fashioned clothing from animal hides. The Cherokees used tree barks and the roots, leaves, and berries of plants to make medicines to treat injuries and disease.

North Carolina's coastal Indians often built walls around their villages for protection.

TALKING TO THE ANIMALS

Telling stories has always been a sacred part of Cherokee life. Here is a tale explaining how the world came to be as it is.

Long ago, in the days before white people came to the mountains, life was peaceful and happy. Humans and animals lived together as friends. Each night, they sat around the campfire and told stories. The snakes talked about the things they saw while crawling through caves. The wolves told about life in the valleys and clearings. The bears shared their adventures of hunting for honey along the mountainsides. And the human beings talked about making pots and building houses in the villages.

As the years passed, the people began to spend more time talking about their own lives—and less time listening to the animals' stories. "They never hear anything I have to say," hissed the snake. "All they want to do is hear themselves talk," howled the wolf. "It's an insult," roared the bear. "Let's leave here and never come back!" None of the humans heard what the animals said. They were much too busy talking to each other. And none of them noticed as the animals left the campsite and wandered into the woods.

Many years later, a large bear walked into the humans' village. "Good morning," said a woman walking by. "Roar," said the bear. "I can't understand you," said the woman. "Let me take you to our chief. I'm sure he'll know what you have to say." But neither the chief nor anyone else in the village could understand the bear. Finally, the bear wandered back into the woods.

A few days later, a young man was chosen to go and live with the animals and learn their language. When he returned to the village many years later, he could hiss like a snake, howl like a wolf, and roar like a bear. He could also share the animals' stories in human words that the other villagers could understand. And this is how the storyteller learned to talk to the animals.

EUROPEANS ARRIVE

In 1524, the first Europeans arrived in the region that would later become North Carolina. With the French flag flying from his mast, an Italian explorer named Giovanni da Verrazano sailed along the coastline. He traveled from the area near the Cape Fear River on the southern shore all the way to the northern corner of what is now North Carolina. During the next fifty years, a number of Spanish explorers led expeditions north from Florida into the area. But neither France nor Spain set up a colony.

During the 1580s, the North Carolina coastline became the site of England's first colonies in the New World. Sir Walter Raleigh,

Sir Walter Raleigh financed colonies on Roanoke Island in 1585 and 1587. They were the first English settlements in the New World.

who had been granted the land by Queen Elizabeth, sent two expeditions to the area. Little is known about the first settlement. It was established on Roanoke Island in 1585 and quickly failed.

Two years later, a second group of settlers, led by John White, arrived at Roanoke Island. Shortly after they arrived, a little girl named Virginia Dare was born. She was the first child born to English-speaking parents in the New World.

The new colonists made their homes in the wooden houses left behind from the first settlement. They quickly made friends with the Indians who lived in the area. But the settlers had difficulty surviving off the resources available on the island. White soon returned to England to get more food and supplies.

For almost three years, war between England and Spain made it impossible for White to return to the colony. When he finally returned to Roanoke Island in 1590, he discovered that the colony had been abandoned. No trace remained of the settlers he had left behind less than three years earlier. The only clue he could find was the single word *Croatoan*, which was carved in huge letters on a tree.

THE SOUTHERN PLANTATION

Not until the 1650s did English settlements finally gain a foothold in the region. During that period, a steady flow of settlers from southeastern Virginia moved into the northeast corner of what would become North Carolina. The new villages became known as the Southern Plantation, to distinguish them from the English colonies that already existed in Virginia.

In 1663, King Charles presented the Southern Plantation as a gift to eight men who, called the lords proprietors, had helped him come to power. Their property stretched all the way from Virginia to the Spanish colony of Florida, including much of present-day North and South Carolina.

From the beginning, the lords proprietors had problems governing the colony. There were frequent arguments with Virginia over land. And a dreaded pirate known as Blackbeard constantly attacked supply ships off the coast. But the most serious conflict was with the Tuscaroras, who lived along the Neuse River. Chief Hancock of the Tuscaroras was angry with the white settlers for building homes and farms on his tribe's land. In 1711, the Indians attacked an English settlement near present-day New Bern, killing sixty people. During the next year, the Europeans and Tuscaroras fought one battle after another. After their defeat, the Tuscaroras fled north to New York.

In 1729, all but one of the lords proprietors sold their holdings back to England, and Carolina became a royal colony. The colony was governed by the same laws as under the lords proprietors, but now the British king was the one who appointed the governor and other colonial officials.

SLAVERY AND THE QUAKERS

During the 1740s and 1750s, a group of English settlers known as the Quakers moved from Pennsylvania into the Piedmont region of North Carolina. Most settled near what would become Greensboro. Then, in 1753, a German religious group called the Moravians founded the village of Salem. In the following years, waves of German settlers from Pennsylvania migrated into the area,

In this painting by Mary Lyed Hicks Williams, slaves gather straw. Although the life of slaves was always harsh, it became worse after 1831, when the North Carolina legislature outlawed slaves' social gatherings and black-led churches in an attempt to prevent slave revolts.

building tiny breweries, sawmills, and tanneries. The Quakers and the Moravians believed that everyone should have the right to worship in any way that they pleased. They also believe that all people—regardless of the color of their skin—were equal in the eyes of God.

African slaves had first arrived in North Carolina with the earliest European explorers and settlers. As large tobacco and cotton plantations sprang up along the southern coast and around Charlotte, more and more slaves were brought into the region. Slaves worked from sunrise to sunset each day, clearing the land and planting and picking the crops.

Visiting North Carolina in 1747, the Quaker missionary John Woolman was deeply troubled by the conditions under which the slaves lived and worked. "I saw so many vices and corruptions increased by this slave trade and this way of life," he wrote, "that it appeared to me as a dark gloominess hanging over the land." Through his preaching and writing, Woolman convinced many Quaker settlers to free their slaves and to speak out against slavery.

A NEW NATION

As the years passed, North Carolinians came to resent being ruled by a governor they had not elected. In western North Carolina, a group calling themselves the Regulators began to openly protest British rule of the colony. In 1775, people in western North Carolina signed a document called the Mecklenburg Declaration of Independence, expressing their desire to be free from England. The movement for independence soon spread all across the colony. On July 15, 1775, North Carolina's last colonial governor, Josiah Martin, returned to England on a British warship after he was chased from the colony by a group of angry patriots. Eight years later, at the end of the Revolutionary War, North Carolina found itself part of a new nation.

In 1828, former North Carolina resident Andrew Jackson was elected U.S. president. One of the young nation's most celebrated military leaders, he had became a national hero during the War of 1812. Jackson harbored a bitter hatred for Native Americans. While

ON THE AFFAIR BETWEEN THE REBEL GENERALS HOWE AND GADDESDEN

During the American Revolution, North Carolina–born general Robert Howe was put in command of the southern Continental forces. This was met with great disapproval in South Carolina. Howe's unpopularity was in part due to his bitter rivalry with South Carolina's General Christopher Gadsden (spelled differently in the song). The affair reached such a pitch that the two actually fought a duel—which, though bloodless, calmed things down between them.

Words By Major John André **Music: "Yankee Doodle"**

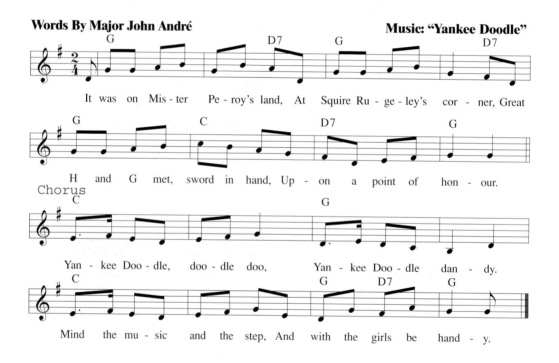

It was on Mis - ter Pe - roy's land, At Squire Ru - ge - ley's cor - ner, Great H and G met, sword in hand, Up - on a point of hon - our.

Chorus

Yan - kee Doo - dle, doo - dle doo, Yan - kee Doo - dle dan - dy.

Mind the mu - sic and the step, And with the girls be hand - y.

They met, and in the usual way,
With hat in hand saluted,
Which was, no doubt, to show how they
Like Gentleman disputed *Chorus*

And then they both made
This honest declaration,
That they came there—by honor led,
But—not by inclination. *Chorus*

That if they fought, 'twas not because
Of rancour, spite or passion,
But only to obey the laws
Of custom and of fashion. *Chorus*

The pistols then, before their eyes,
were fairly prim'd and loaded!
H wish'd, and so did G likewise,
The custom was exploded. *Chorus*

But as they now had gone so far
In such a bloody business,
For action straight they both prepar'd
With—mutual forgiveness. *Chorus*

Quoth H to G—Sir, please to fire,
Quoth G—no, pray begin, Sir;
And truly, one must needs admire
The temper they were in, Sir! *Chorus*

We'll fire both at once, said he,
And so they both presented;
No answer was returned by G,
But silence, Sir, consented. *Chorus*

They paus'd a while, these gallant foes,
By turns politely grinning,
Till after many cons and pros,
H made a brisk beginning. *Chorus*

He miss'd his mark, but not his aim,
The shot was well directed;
It sav'd them both from hurt and shame;
What more could be expected! *Chorus*

Then G, to show he meant no harm,
But hated jars and jangles,
His pistol fired, across his arm,
From H—almost at angles. *Chorus*

H now was call'd upon by G
To fire another shot, Sir,
He smil'd, and,—"after this," quoth he,
"No, truly, I cannot, Sir." *Chorus*

Such honour they did both display,
They highly were commended;
And thus, in short, this gallant fray
Without mischance was ended. *Chorus*

No fresh dispute, we may suppose,
Will e'er by them be started,
For now the Chiefs, no longer foes,
Shook hands, and—so they parted. *Chorus*

president, he drove the nation's original inhabitants farther and farther west. In 1838, President Martin Van Buren ordered U.S. troops to remove the Cherokees from their homes in western North Carolina, fulfilling Jackson's plan to clear the area of its original inhabitants. The Cherokees were forced to relocate to a reservation in Oklahoma. Suffering from cold, disease, and starvation, many Cherokees died during the thousand-mile journey that became known as the Trail of Tears. But hundreds of Cherokees

A quarter of the Cherokee who made the trip along the Trail of Tears from their homes in the East to Oklahoma died along the way.

avoided capture and escaped into the North Carolina hills, where they continued to live.

THE CIVIL WAR

By the 1850s, slavery had already begun to disappear in North Carolina. There were very few slaves in the mountains or along the coast. In the Piedmont, where slavery was more common, the Quakers and Moravians had convinced many of their neighbors to free their slaves. North Carolina's Quakers and Moravians had also become leaders in the Underground Railroad, a string of hiding places where runaway slaves could stay on their way to freedom in the North.

In 1861, the long-simmering dispute between Northern and Southern states erupted into civil war. When the war began, the majority of North Carolinians still supported the Union. But when President Abraham Lincoln commanded the North Carolina militia to fight against the rebellious troops in South Carolina, North Carolina's position quickly changed. Whatever their feelings about slavery, most North Carolinians were not willing to go to war against their Southern neighbors. "I can be no party to this wicked violation of the Constitution," said Governor John Willis Ellis, in defiance of Lincoln's orders. "You can get no troops from North Carolina."

The North Carolina legislature soon voted to secede from the Union and join the other slaveholding states in the newly formed Confederate States of America. In the next four years the state supplied more than 125,000 men to the Confederate army—more

Union general William Tecumseh Sherman meets Confederate general Joseph Johnston following the Union victory at Bentonville, the last major battle of the Civil War.

than any other state. North Carolina also suffered three times as many casualties as any other state. On April 26, 1865, Confederate general Joseph Johnston surrendered to Union general William Tecumseh Sherman near Durham. It was the last major battle of the Civil War.

THE WAR'S AFTERMATH

Only a few days earlier, President Lincoln had been killed by an assassin's bullet. Vice President Andrew Johnson, a North Carolina native, was sworn in as president. Johnson attempted to restore the nation to unity, but many Northern politicians resented his forgiving stance toward the South. In 1868, the U.S. House of Representatives voted that Johnson should face impeachment—a trial held by the U.S. Senate to determine if he should be removed from office. Although the Senate did not vote to remove Johnson, he will forever be remembered as the first president to be impeached.

In a curious twist of fate, the Civil War contributed to the long-term development of North Carolina's economy. Throughout the war, soldiers were given chewing tobacco along with food. Many of these men had never used tobacco before, but once they had tried it, they continued to buy it after the war. With all the new tobacco buyers, tobacco farming and production became a serious business in North Carolina. In 1874, Washington Duke and his sons built their first tobacco factory in Durham. The following year, R. J. Reynolds founded his own tobacco company in Winston-Salem. In the decades that followed, North Carolina would become one of the world's leading tobacco producers.

After gaining their freedom, most former slaves decided to remain in the state. Many continued to work on the small farms and plantations of their former masters. Others took jobs working on tobacco farms or in tobacco factories. But while jobs were plentiful for the freed slaves, life was hard and freedom was severely limited. During the 1870s, a group of laws, known as the Black Code, was passed by the all-white state legislature. These laws prevented African Americans from holding office or owning property. African Americans in North Carolina would continue to suffer under the influence of these racist laws for almost one hundred years.

Although the Civil War ended slavery in North Carolina, most former slaves continued to live in dire poverty, often working for their former owners.

MOVING FORWARD

During the twentieth century, North Carolinians have overcome hardship and conflict to improve the quality of life in their state. In 1901, Governor Charles B. Aycock formed North Carolina's first public school system. At the time, most people in the state worked on farms. And most school-age children spent almost nine months of the year working alongside their parents harvesting tobacco,

FIRST IN FLIGHT

In 1900, two brothers from Dayton, Ohio, named Orville and Wilbur Wright began trying to build the world's first motorized flying machine. Unable to get their winged inventions off the ground, the Wright brothers began searching for a place with the best wind conditions for flying. After a lengthy search, they chose a sandy, isolated area called Kitty Hawk, in northeastern North Carolina. In 1902, the brothers successfully tested a motorless glider, sailing 620 feet over the sandy dunes. The following year, they returned to Kitty Hawk. Only this time, the original glider sported a front-end propeller that was powered by a four-cylinder, twelve-horsepower engine. On December 17, Wilbur tried unsuccessfully to get the new machine off the ground at Kill Devil Hills, a few miles from Kitty Hawk. A few minutes later, Orville gave the machine a second try. The whole trip lasted only twelve seconds, and the primitive airplane traveled only 120 feet before it came back to Earth. But the Wright brothers had proven—once and for all—that humans could use motorized machines to fly through the air. The age of air travel had officially begun.

corn, or cotton. Only one out of three children attended school at all. Over the next few decades, hundreds of new schools were built and thousands of new teachers were hired throughout the state. North Carolina slowly began to transform itself from a largely illiterate state to a leader in education and literacy in the Southeast.

During the 1920s, North Carolina began a pioneer road-building program. The hundreds of dirt roads that crisscrossed the state were gradually paved. The new program earned North Carolina the nickname the Good Roads State. Thanks to this program, even

POPULATION GROWTH: 1800–2000

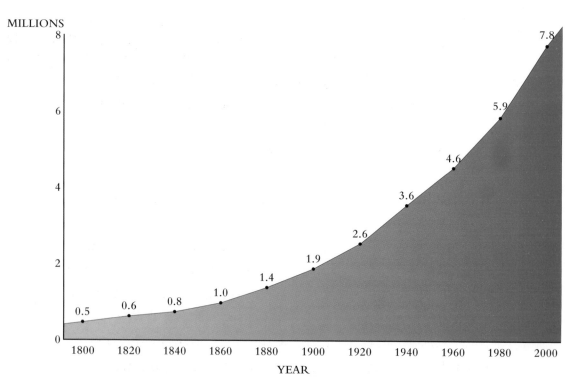

North Carolina paved hundreds of dirt roads in the 1920s, making it easier to get to many of the state's isolated towns.

today the state has the second-largest system of state-maintained roads in the nation.

In the late 1920s, the nation's economy collapsed in what is known as the Great Depression. People were left without jobs or money as businesses shut down and farm prices dropped. North Carolina suffered along with the rest of the nation.

But this was also an important time of growth for the state, as the federal government stepped in with construction projects to put people back to work. Along the coast, thousands of North Carolinians were employed digging the canals that formed the Intracoastal Waterway. Meanwhile, workers in western North Carolina built two important routes through the mountains. Begun in the early 1930s, the Blue Ridge Parkway provides millions of travelers with breathtaking views of the North Carolina mountains each year. And the scenic mountain pathways of the Appalachian Trail, which was completed in 1933, help make the Smoky and Blue Ridge Mountains among the most popular vacation areas in the nation.

THE CIVIL RIGHTS MOVEMENT

For many years, North Carolina's growing prosperity did not include all its citizens. Almost one hundred years after the Civil War, African Americans still did not enjoy the same rights and freedoms as their white neighbors.

In 1960, four college students in Greensboro staged a protest that would change life in North Carolina forever. At the time, most white-owned restaurants in the state refused to serve blacks. The teenagers decided to challenge the practice. On February 1, they sat down at the lunch counter of the Woolworth store in downtown Greensboro and asked to see menus. But the Woolworth employees refused to serve the young men. During the days that followed, more and more people joined the group—including several white students from the area. This form of protest, called a sit-in, soon spread to other restaurants and stores. A few days later, with television cameras rolling, the young people were finally served their meals. After that, white-owned businesses throughout the state began to open their doors to black customers. "I was tired of just talking about equal rights," Franklin McCain, one of the students, remembered many years later. "This is my country. No one's going to deny me the opportunity. I'm going to be a full participant of every aspect of this community."

The ongoing struggle for racial equality in North Carolina has not always been easy. In 1971, African-American students were protesting segregation, or the separation of races, in the Wilmington schools. After a grocery store was burned down, ten young people were arrested. Many people believed that the teenagers, who became known as the Wilmington Ten, were innocent and had only been suspects because of their involvement in the protests. All ten were convicted, however, and received prison sentences of at least twenty years. But in 1979, the three main witnesses against them confessed that they had lied, and the following year, the Wilmington Ten were released from prison.

In recent years, North Carolinians have struggled to bring prosperity and freedom to all citizens. From the colonists who fought for independence to the protesters in Greensboro, North Carolinians have made great sacrifices to improve the quality of life in their state. "We still have a long way to go," reflects a teacher in Wilmington, "but we've come so far in this state. Somehow, we always seem to be at our best when there's a challenge to face. And I'm a strong believer that North Carolina will continue to grow and to prosper."

3 A GOVERNMENT FOR ALL

The capitol in Raleigh

North Carolina has traditionally been home to two very different groups of people. The residents of the state's rapidly growing urban areas usually vote for Democratic candidates. They support a strong role for the government in providing health care, education, and equal opportunity for all the state's citizens. The people who make their homes in the state's small towns and rustic farmlands are more likely to vote for Republicans. They think that their religious beliefs should serve as a guide for the laws governing the state. Over the years, North Carolina's government has reflected this diversity and competing needs of its people.

INSIDE GOVERNMENT

North Carolina's government is divided into three branches: executive, legislative, and judicial.

Executive. The governor heads North Carolina's executive branch. He or she is responsible for appointing important officials and introducing new policies in areas such as education, health care, and law enforcement. The governor is elected to a four-year term. Other officials in North Carolina's executive branch include the lieutenant governor, the state treasurer, and the attorney general.

Legislative. The North Carolina legislature is divided into two houses: a senate with 50 members and a house of representatives

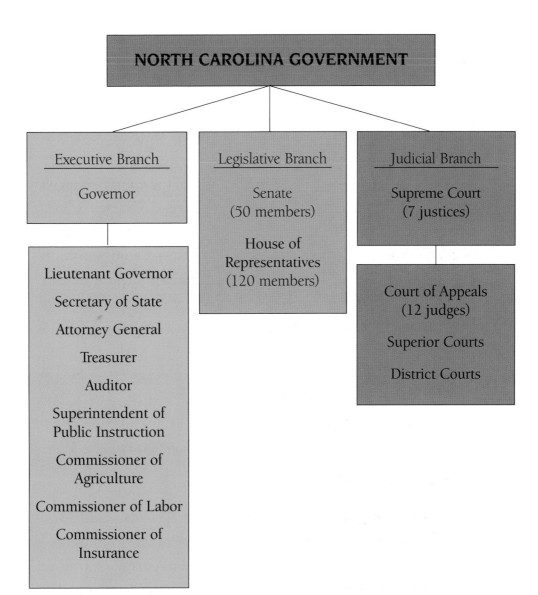

NORTH CAROLINA GOVERNMENT

Executive Branch

Governor

Lieutenant Governor

Secretary of State

Attorney General

Treasurer

Auditor

Superintendent of
Public Instruction

Commissioner of
Agriculture

Commissioner of Labor

Commissioner of
Insurance

Legislative Branch

Senate
(50 members)

House of
Representatives
(120 members)

Judicial Branch

Supreme Court
(7 justices)

Court of Appeals
(12 judges)

Superior Courts

District Courts

with 120 members. Members of both houses are elected to two-year terms. The legislature is responsible for introducing and passing the bills that will become state laws. After a majority of the members in both houses pass a bill, it is signed by the governor and becomes law.

Judicial. Most trials in North Carolina are held in superior or district courts. District courts hear cases involving minor crimes and civil suits. Superior courts try more serious cases. Whenever someone disagrees with a decision in one of the state's trial courts, the case is sent to the court of appeals to decide whether the decision should be upheld or overruled. If the decision of the court of appeals is also challenged, the North Carolina Supreme Court, the state's highest court, reviews the case. It has the final say in the matter.

All North Carolina judges are elected. The seven supreme court justices, twelve court of appeals judges, and all superior court judges are elected to eight-year terms. District court judges serve four-year terms.

DEMOCRAT AND REPUBLICAN

Politics has always been explosive in North Carolina. People often disagree sharply over how the state should be governed.

For almost one hundred years after the Civil War, Democrats controlled politics in North Carolina. In the late 1960s, however, many citizens—particularly people from small towns and rural areas—began to speak out against the views of the Democratic Party. During this period, some Democrats took strong stands in favor of greater rights for African Americans and against the Vietnam War. Over time, conservative North Carolinians who opposed these positions began voting for Republican candidates in greater and greater numbers. Today the state is evenly divided between urban centers like Charlotte, Raleigh, and Winston-Salem—where Democrats are still a majority—and the primarily Republican rural areas and small towns.

Urban and rural North Carolinians often have different viewpoints on politics and social issues. "I've lived both here in the city and in a small town up in the mountains," says a retired minister in Raleigh, "and it breaks my heart to see people so angry at each other. But I truly believe both sides really love this state."

BLACK AND WHITE

Race plays an important part in the life of North Carolina's citizens. Most people—both black and white—agree that North Carolina has made great strides since the 1960s in providing freedom and opportunity for all its people.

JESSE HELMS: A CONSERVATIVE HERO

No politician represents the attitudes of rural and small town North Carolinians better than Republican senator Jesse Helms. Helms first became popular in the 1960s as a radio and television commentator who spoke out against the civil rights movement and the student protests of the Vietnam War. In 1972, Helms was elected to the U.S. Senate, a position he still holds. Over the years, his strong conservative stands—supporting prayer in public schools and opposing abortion, for instance—have made him a beloved folk hero among conservatives in the state. These same views have made him a hated villain among moderates and liberals in the cities.

Every six years, Helms's campaigns divide North Carolina into two opposing camps. The state is so evenly divided, in fact, that Senator Helms has triumphed in his recent runs for the Senate by the narrowest of margins.

"You either love Jesse or you hate him," explains a merchant in Asheville. "There's just no middle ground with folks here. Show me someone who says that they don't have a strong opinion about Senator Jesse Helms, and I'll bet you that person has never spent a day in North Carolina."

ETHNIC NORTH CAROLINA

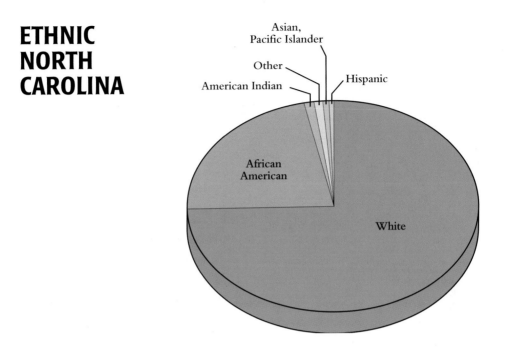

Black and white North Carolinians have had a much harder time learning to get along on a personal level. One of the biggest problems has been where people live. Most African Americans live in the Piedmont region and the northern coastal plain. Meanwhile, people who live in the western mountains are almost exclusively white. Because of this, many black and white North Carolinians have very little contact with each other.

This lack of contact sometimes leads to misunderstanding and suspicion. In recent years, blacks and whites have often found themselves on opposite sides of political debates. While most whites in the state regularly vote Republican, African Americans are much more likely to vote Democratic. Racial divisions have played an important role in the last two campaigns involving Senator Jesse

More than 20 percent of North Carolinians are African Americans. Most live in the Piedmont or along the coast.

Helms. Designed to appeal to rural and small town white voters, Helms's campaign ads have accused the Democratic Party of catering to the interests of black voters. Ads for his opponents, meanwhile, have accused Helms and his followers of prejudice against African Americans.

"Sometimes it seems like blacks and whites in this state live in completely different worlds," says an African American in Chapel Hill. "We're constantly struggling to find ways to talk to each other and to understand each other. But we just live so far apart and seem to have so little in common. I don't think things will ever really change till we find some way to spend more time together."

FROM FARMS TO FACTORIES

North Carolina enjoys one of the most successful economies in the nation. It leads the southeastern states in both agriculture and industry. The state's pleasant climate also encourages tourism and outdoor recreation, like hiking, boating, and golf, which play an important role in the economy.

North Carolina's economy has changed in recent years. The state is no longer primarily agricultural. Today, most people live in cities or towns, working in offices or factories. Real estate, health services,

GROSS STATE PRODUCT: $227.6 BILLION

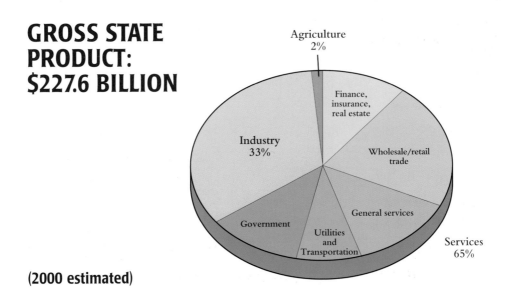

Agriculture 2%

Finance, insurance, real estate

Industry 33%

Wholesale/retail trade

General services

Government

Utilities and Transportation

Services 65%

(2000 estimated)

and chemical production have joined textiles, tobacco, and construction as the state's largest businesses.

Today, the manufacturing of textiles such as fabrics, yarns, threads, and clothing is the state's leading industry. North Carolina leads the nation in textile production. North Carolina also leads the nation in its second-largest industry, the manufacturing of cigarettes and other tobacco products. More than half of the cigarettes purchased each year in the United States are produced and packaged in the state.

Hiking in the misty forests of the Great Smoky Mountains is one of the many activities that lure tourists to North Carolina.

Producing textiles is
North Carolina's biggest
industry.

Tobacco has been important to
North Carolina's economy since
the Civil War.

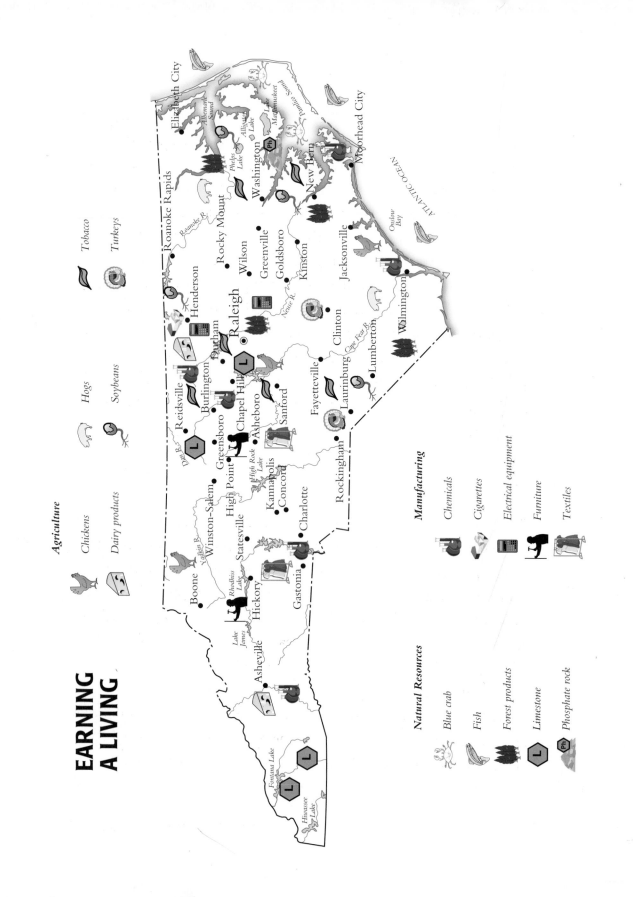

EARNING A LIVING

Agriculture

Chickens
Dairy products
Hogs
Soybeans
Tobacco
Turkeys

Manufacturing

Chemicals
Cigarettes
Electrical equipment
Furniture
Textiles

Natural Resources

Blue crab
Fish
Forest products
Limestone
Phosphate rock

Elizabeth City
Moorhead City
Albemarle Sound
Pamlico Sound
Lake Mattamuskeet
Alligator Lake
Phelps Lake
Washington
New Bern
Roanoke Rapids
Rocky Mount
Wilson
Greenville
Goldsboro
Kinston
Jacksonville
Onslow Bay
ATLANTIC OCEAN
Roanoke R.
Henderson
Raleigh
Durham
Neuse R.
Clinton
Wilmington
Lumberton
Cape Fear R.
Fayetteville
Laurinburg
Reidsville
Burlington
Chapel Hill
Asheboro
Sanford
Greensboro
Dan R.
High Point
High Rock Lake
Kannapolis
Concord
Rockingham
Winston-Salem
Statesville
Charlotte
Boone
Yadkin R.
Rhodhiss Lake
Hickory
Gastonia
Lake James
Asheville
Fontana Lake
Hiwassee Lake

The R. J. Reynolds Tobacco Company in Winston-Salem operates two of the world's largest facilities. North Carolina also ranks first nationwide in the production of wooden household furniture. Other important industries in the state include the manufacture of chemicals, computers, and electronic equipment.

In the last half-century, North Carolina has become known as a center of research on everything from high technology to chemicals. Much of it is done at the Research Triangle Park between Raleigh and Durham. The Research Triangle was founded in 1958 as a collaboration between Duke University, the University of North Carolina at Chapel Hill, North Carolina State University, and several local businesses. Today, it houses the largest collection of research-based businesses in the country. Each morning, more than 43,000 people go to work there.

AGRICULTURE

Despite the emphasis on manufacturing, technology, and service industries, agriculture still plays an important role in North Carolina's economy. The state has more farms than any other southeastern state. The state's chief agricultural product is tobacco. Each year, North Carolina raises nearly two-fifths of the nation's tobacco crop. Corn, cotton, and peanuts are also important crops.

In recent years, raising cattle for both beef and dairy products has become increasingly important to the state's economy. Other valuable agricultural products are chickens, turkeys, fruits, and sweet potatoes. Tree nurseries abound in the mountains and on the coastal plain, where millions of seedlings are grown each year.

Fishing is another important source of income in the state, especially in coastal waters. Flounder, sea trout, and croaker are the most popular catches, along with crabs, oysters, clams, and shrimps.

HOLLYWOOD EAST

In the past two decades, film production has become big business in North Carolina, particularly in Wilmington. Today, so many film companies and production crews are active in the area that it is known as Hollywood East. Such famous films as *Blue Velvet* and *Virus* have been filmed there. The area also provides the scenic setting for the popular television series *Dawson's Creek*.

A fisherman shows off his impressive blue crab catch.

HAMS AND YAMS

Although North Carolina is no longer the agricultural state it once was, many people are committed to preserving the memory of the old rural way of life. Smithfield's Ham and Yam Festival is one of the tastiest ways to experience a bit of it.

Each year, more sweet potatoes (also known as yams) are grown in the fields around Smithfield in Johnston County than anywhere else in the nation. A highlight of the festival is the yam-cooking contest. The yams can be prepared however the contestant chooses—baked, sugar-coated, pureed or french-fried. But whatever the recipe, the yams must have been grown in Johnston County.

Johnston County is also famed for its delicious hams. For years, the festival has included a contest between cooks in Smithfield and their counterparts in Smithfield, Virginia, to see who could prepare the tastiest ham. Today, the ham-cooking contest includes cooks from across North Carolina.

Besides all the good eating, the festival features exhibits about farm life and rural arts and crafts. "It's really a wonderful opportunity to show young people how most of us used to live," says a teacher from Raleigh who brings her children to the festival each year. "It's something that's so easy to forget. But the taste of that ham and those sweet yams—that's something you'll never forget."

So why has Wilmington become so appealing to film and television producers? "I guess Wilmington is as close as we can get to the American Dream. It's a real Norman Rockwell kind of town," says Mark Stricklin, director of the Wilmington Film Commission, referring to the painter famous for his sentimental scenes of small town life. "In this day and age, that's pretty attractive."

4
PRIDE AND COMPETITION

North Carolinians have always loved competition. The state's athletes often perform at a level that inspires fans around the state and beyond. But competition in North Carolina extends far beyond the sporting arena. The state is famous for its bluegrass music festivals, in which talented instrumentalists trade solos with the same fierce intensity as prizefighters. North Carolina's competitive spirit also extends into public life, where bitterly fought religious controversies sometimes pit moderates against fundamentalists.

SPORTS

There are few things that North Carolinians care more about than sports. Richard and Lee Petty, a father and son who dominated stock car racing for more than three decades, are both from Randolph County. The state is filled with racing fans who have followed the careers of the Pettys and other local racers. North Carolina's magnificent golf courses are popular destinations for golfers from around the country. The rolling meadows of the Sandhills boast more than forty golf courses, including the Pinehurst Country Club, where the prestigious U.S. Open golf tournament is sometimes held. And since the Carolina Panthers came to Charlotte, North Carolinians have begun to develop an enthusiasm for professional football.

The biggest sports attraction in North Carolina, however, is college basketball. In recent years, five different North Carolina colleges have made the NCAA tournament, which determines the best team in college basketball.

During the past twenty-five years, the state has been split by the heated competition between North Carolina's two most successful teams—the Duke Blue Devils and the Tar Heels of the University of North Carolina at Chapel Hill. These two teams have had more than their share of outstanding players, but the real heroes in

North Carolinians are so crazy about stock car racing that the local news gives the results of any race entered by local drivers.

A Carolina Panthers fan shows her true colors.

Carolina basketball are the coaches. During the 1980s and 1990s, Chapel Hill's Dean Smith and Duke's Mike Krzyzewski were probably the two most popular and respected men in the state. Almost every year during that period, one of the coaches led his team into the Final Four, in which the nation's top four teams compete for the championship. Each man's team has won two national championships.

Although the two schools are less than ten miles apart, their fans are bitterly divided. Each spring, people throughout the state find themselves cheering passionately for one team—and cheering just as passionately against the other. Family members and close friends get into heated arguments about which of the two teams has the best players, the best coach, and the best fans. "There's just no middle ground when it comes to Duke and Carolina," explains a minister from the Asheville area who is a devoted Tar Heel fan. "People hate one and love the other. During the tournament especially, you'll see sane, responsible people, who are normally kind and respectful of one another, rooting just as loudly for the other team to lose as they do for their own team to win. And if you want me to be honest about it, I'm the same way. It's really kind of embarrassing if you think about it."

RELIGION

Religion is central in the lives of most North Carolinians. The vast majority of the state's citizens are Christian, and most of them can be seen heading to Protestant services each Sunday morning, dressed in their finest clothing. The best-known religious leader in the United States during the past forty years, Baptist minister Billy Graham, makes his home in the tiny mountain town of Montreat, about twenty miles south of Asheville.

While North Carolinians agree about the importance of religion in their lives, they often disagree about what they believe. People in rural parts of the state tend to be conservative in their religious beliefs. Most conservative Protestants, called fundamentalists, believe that the Bible is literally true and that there is only one way to interpret it. They also feel that the Bible should be taught in public schools and that men—and not women—should be the leaders in the church, the family, and society at large. "What we believe may not be popular with everyone," says a conservative minister in Winston-Salem. "But the Bible teaches what it teaches, and it's important that everyone has the chance to hear it."

Protestants in the Piedmont and in urban areas and college towns tend to be more moderate or liberal in their religious beliefs. Moderate Protestants believe that the Bible can be interpreted in different ways. They feel that personal religious beliefs should not be practiced in schools and that women should join men as leaders in all areas of life. "For me, it's less about quoting a particular passage from the Bible and more about living my life

On Sunday mornings, you'll find many North Carolinians in church.

in the spirit that the Bible reveals," says a Raleigh resident. "I think if we spent less time arguing about what the Bible says and more time living what it teaches, the world would be a much better place."

Over the years, conservative and moderate Christians in North Carolina have disagreed over a number of issues. On several occasions, Baptist leaders have challenged Wake Forest University, which was founded by Southern Baptists, for certain policies, such as serving alcohol on campus. But the most bitter controversy in recent years involved Southeastern Baptist Theological Seminary in Wake Forest. In the early 1980s, fundamentalists took control of the board of trustees of the traditionally moderate seminary. Within a few years, almost all the faculty members had been replaced with more conservative teachers.

"The thing about being from North Carolina," explains a South-eastern Seminary graduate, "is that no matter how much you may disagree with someone, you still have a common ground as fellow North Carolinians. I think that's what's different about what happened at Southeastern. Once the new people took over, there wasn't any room to disagree any more. But I suspect that will change one day soon. We here in North Carolina have strong opinions and we often disagree with each other, but we somehow always seem to find that common ground."

BLUEGRASS AND BEACH MUSIC

Music is another thing North Carolinians feel strongly about—and are opinionated about as well.

For people in the western part of the state, the traditional music called bluegrass is often the music of choice. Bluegrass music began in Kentucky in 1938, when mandolin player Bill Monroe formed his band, the Blue Grass Boys. As perfected by Monroe, bluegrass combined the mournful melodies of African-American blues with the lyrics and instrumental styles of traditional Irish, Scottish, and English folk music. From its earliest days, bluegrass was character-ized by the astonishing skill and blistering speed of the musicians who played it.

Bluegrass may have gotten its start in Kentucky, but the moun-tain people of western North Carolina quickly put their own stamp on it. In the years before bluegrass, Spray native Charlie Poole developed a new style of banjo playing—by plucking the instru-ment one note at a time with his fingers—that would later have an enormous impact on bluegrass. Flint Hill native Earl Scruggs took Charlie Poole's banjo technique and turned it into an art form. In the 1950s, Doc Watson, a blind musician from the tiny township of Stoney Fork, transformed the guitar from a rhythm instrument into a solo instrument with a new style of playing called flat-picking. "I tell you," enthuses an accountant from Asheville, "seeing Doc Watson on stage is something you're never likely to forget. . . . It's total concentration and absolute joy. He shuts his eyes tight and his head rocks into the rhythm of the song—and those fingers of his move so fast across the face of that guitar that you can hardly see them any more. If you love music, there's just nothing like it anywhere."

Today, bluegrass is still very much alive in North Carolina. Each spring and summer, thousands of people attend bluegrass festivals

No bluegrass band is complete without a banjo player.

all across the state. But the granddaddy of bluegrass festivals—in North Carolina or anywhere else—is the Ole Time Fiddler's & Bluegrass Festival, which is held in the sleepy little community of Union Grove. Over the years, the nation's finest bluegrass musicians have saved their most spirited performances for the fans from around the world who crowd into Union Grove during the last weekend in May. For the more adventuresome fans, the festival also offers lessons on playing—and making—bluegrass instruments, such as mandolins, guitars, and hammer dulcimers.

At the other end of the state, people along the shore spend their springs and summers listening—and dancing—to another type of music. Locals call it beach music.

The beach music tradition began during the early 1970s, when a smooth style of African-American music called rhythm and blues became popular at dances and beach parties along the coast. To local beachcombers, the music's soft, shuffling rhythms seemed perfect for dancing barefoot in the sand in the moonlight. Before long, local bands filled out their sets with classic rhythm-and-blues tunes from the 1950s and 1960s, and local songwriters began writing new songs with the same smooth rhythms and wistful lyrics as the old ones. Soon, many visitors were coming to the area just to hear the music.

Today, beach music concerts are commonplace along the North Carolina shore, and beach music festivals have begun popping up. The biggest is the Crystal Coast Beach Music Festival, held in mid-May. Each year, thousands of beach music fans pile into the community to hear such classic beach music performers as the Chairmen of the Board, the Embers, and Captain Cook and the Coconuts.

NORTH CAROLINA'S FAVORITE FOOD

North Carolina's most enduring contribution to American cooking is its unique style of pit-cooked pork barbecue. To achieve the

The Union Grove bluegrass festival is a great place to hear lively music or pick up a new violin.

Lexington is considered the barbecue capital of North Carolina. The little town has joint after joint serving up pork roasted over a wood fire.

distinctive taste and smell, a pig is roasted in a deep pit over a wood or charcoal flame. The meat is lightly covered with a "dry sauce," which is usually made with vinegar, hot peppers, and sugar.

Almost everyone in the state has an opinion about how to make the best barbecue. Most North Carolinians have little patience for

outsiders who prefer the meat cooked in other barbecue hotbeds such as Texas or Memphis, Tennessee. "There's only one way to make barbecue," boasts a factory foreman from Zebulon, "and that's the way we make it here. Who do people think they're kidding with all that heavy sauce they put on their meat? If the meat is cooked

EASTERN NORTH CAROLINA BARBECUE SAUCE

The most important thing about barbecue sauce is finding the taste that's right for you. This simple recipe should allow you to add and mix ingredients until you find just the right taste. Have an adult help you with the cooking.

1 quart of vinegar
¼ cup of salt
½ tablespoon of red pepper
1 tablespoon of red pepper flakes
¼ cup of packed brown sugar (or ½ cup of honey)

Stir all the ingredients together. Taste. Add additional pepper, salt, or sugar until it tastes just the way you like it. Let the entire mix stand overnight.

Most North Carolinians prefer their barbecued dishes with very little sauce. But it's really up to you to decide how much—or how little—to use. Cook meat, fish, chicken, tofu, or vegetables over an open grill outdoors. Each time you turn the item over the fire, use a brush or wooden spoon to apply a coat of sauce. Once the food has cooked, add an extra layer of sauce to taste.

right, there's no need to cover it. You just give it a little seasoning to bring out the flavor, and it's ready to eat just like it is."

In fact, North Carolinians themselves tend to disagree, both about how the pork should be cooked and the sauce that should be used to flavor it. Barbecue eaters near the coast prefer to cook the whole pig at once and to baste it with a sharp vinegar-and-pepper sauce that uses no tomatoes. As you move farther west, people tend to cook only the shoulders of the hog and to soften their sauce by adding a light tomato paste to the mix.

The idea of barbecuing an entire hog at once was first introduced in the city of Lexington. Each Saturday afternoon, folks would gather around to watch and wait as two large pigs were slowly barbecued over an open pit dug at the center of the town square. Eventually, the pit was moved inside a wooden shelter with a brick chimney, with a restaurant right beside it. Barbecue joints are still usually small, no-nonsense places, with paper plates and simple wooden tables. And Lexington is still the most popular place in North Carolina to eat barbecue.

5 THE BEST OF THE BEST

Over the years, North Carolina has been home to a remarkable variety of people. From music to journalism, from sports to literature, North Carolinians have had a major impact on almost every field.

AIR JORDAN

No one who has seen Michael Jordan play basketball will ever forget the sight. Jordan raced up and down the court with astonishing speed. He could dart effortlessly past players who tried to defend him. When he came within ten feet of the basket, he would leap high into the air, his eyes wide and his tongue dangling from his mouth. As he sailed across the floor, he would move the ball from one hand to the other. At the last possible second, he would raise the ball above his head with one hand and smash it through the hoop. "Air Jordan" had done it again.

Born in Brooklyn, New York, in 1963, Michael moved with his family to Wilmington, North Carolina, when he was still a small child. In high school he quickly established himself as one of the top young players in the state. During his senior year, he decided to attend the University of North Carolina at Chapel Hill, where he could play for the team's celebrated coach, Dean Smith. In 1981, as a freshman at Chapel Hill, Jordan earned a spot in the team's

"A lot of guys in the NBA are great athletes, but nobody ever had that kid's drive, even in high school," says Ron Coley, one of Michael Jordan's high school coaches.

starting lineup. By the end of the season, Jordan and his talented teammates had captured a national championship.

In 1984, Jordan joined the Chicago Bulls in the National Basketball Association. In his first year with the Bulls, he led the team in scoring, rebounds, steals, and assists, earning the league's Rookie of the Year award. During the next few years, Jordan just kept getting better. And as his performance improved, his team improved along with him. In 1991, the Bulls won a national championship—an achievement they would repeat five more times over the next seven years.

By the time he retired in 1998, Jordan was one of the best-known people in the world. He served as the spokesperson for Nike shoes, introducing his own popular Air Jordan line. Today, many people believe that Jordan is the greatest basketball player of all time—and perhaps the finest athlete to play any professional sport.

A DISTINCTIVE VOICE

The extraordinary singer Nina Simone was born in 1933 in Tryon, North Carolina. As a small child, she displayed remarkable musical talents, singing in the church choir and picking out songs by ear on the piano. As she grew older, her talents continued to develop. At age seventeen, she left for New York City to study at the prestigious Juilliard School of Music.

After graduating, Simone got her first professional job as a singer and pianist in Atlantic City, New Jersey. There she began to attract the attention of music critics. Everyone who heard her was impressed with the strange quality of her deep voice. The dark, husky tones that rose from her throat were somehow both feminine and masculine at the same time. And she would often shift effortlessly from a sweet, gentle way of singing to a rough, bluesy style.

Though Nina's earliest recordings were jazz, she soon became interested in other types of music. Her 1958 single "Little Girl Blue" became a rhythm-and-blues hit. In the early 1960s, she also developed an interest in folk music and protest music. During the next few years, she released many records protesting the treatment of African Americans and the U.S. involvement in the Vietnam War.

Among her fans around the world, Nina Simone is regarded as one of the most inventive singers—and one of the most difficult

Nina Simone once wrote that she wanted her music "to make people feel on a deep level. . . . When you've got the audience hooked, you always know because it's like electricity hanging in the air."

to classify. She is a master of virtually every popular musical form—from jazz and rhythm and blues to folk, pop, and rock and roll.

YOU CAN'T GO HOME AGAIN

Thomas Wolfe, one of the twentieth century's finest novelists, was born in Asheville in 1900. Tall, lanky, and studious, Thomas wanted

Thomas Wolfe with his mother, Julia, who ran a boardinghouse in Asheville that Wolfe described in his novel Look Homeward, Angel.

to be a writer from the time he was a child. He noticed everything around him in his hometown, making observations that would fill his future novels.

Wolfe's first novel, *Look Homeward, Angel*, was published in 1929. Like his later novels, it was lengthy and passionate. Images and ideas seemed to flow effortlessly from the pages. In the book, Wolfe wrote openly about his experiences in Asheville. Though the characters had fictional names, many bore a striking resemblance to the people he had known as a child. Although the novel was immensely popular, many Asheville residents were upset by what they thought was the unflattering way they had been depicted.

Over the next few years, Wolfe poured himself into his writing. In spite of his remarkable gifts, he was legendary for his sloppiness. When inspired by an image or an idea, he rarely stopped to edit or reread what he had written. His manuscripts were sometimes four times the length of an average novel. But his editor, Maxwell Perkins, carefully edited each novel into a form that readers and critics could understand and accept.

In 1935, Wolfe's book of short stories, *From Death to Mourning*, was published. It would be the last work to appear during his lifetime. Wolfe became ill and died in 1938. Two years later, his novel *You Can't Go Home Again* was published. It is considered Wolfe's masterpiece.

THE TRANE

Jazz musician John Coltrane was born in the tiny community of Hamlet in 1926. As a boy, he exhibited tremendous musical

"Coltrane's trademark was his unique sound which bespoke a relentless search for perfection yet was always . . . compellingly passionate and alive," wrote jazz critic Nat Hentoff.

talent—and an inexhaustible desire to learn and improve himself. While other children were playing, John would spend his free time listening to music and practicing the saxophone and clarinet.

At age nineteen, Coltrane moved to Philadelphia, Pennsylvania, where he first heard a spirited new style of jazz called bebop. At this point in his career, there was nothing particularly distinctive about Coltrane's style of playing the saxophone. But he was determined to learn everything he could about his instrument and to make an impact on the world of jazz. Coltrane studied the techniques of the greatest saxophone players, including Charlie Parker, Lester Young, and Coleman Hawkins. He also practiced long hours every day, working to develop his own unique sound.

In 1949, all the hard work finally began to pay off when Coltrane was invited to play in a band headed by the great trumpet player Dizzy Gillespie, one of the founders of bebop. A few years later, Coltrane joined a band headed by another great trumpet player, Miles Davis. At the time, Davis was the most daring and innovative musician in jazz. His new band took jazz in a darker and more experimental direction than Gillespie's. At twenty-nine, Trane, as his fans now called him, suddenly found himself on the cutting edge of jazz.

By 1960, having established himself as the most gifted saxophone player in jazz, Coltrane decided it was time to start his own band. During the next few years, he recorded one jazz masterpiece after another. Much of the music was loud and wildly experimental. As the other musicians attacked their instruments, Coltrane would blast one deafening chord after another on his saxophone, in a wild swirl of sound. As the years passed, his solos became louder and longer—at times lasting as long as forty-five minutes.

But there was also a restrained, gentle side to Coltrane's music. His renditions of "My Favorite Things" and "My One and Only

Love," along with his recordings of his own compositions "Naima" and "Central Park West," are among the most beautiful performances in the history of jazz. In 1964, Coltrane released what most people consider his finest recording, "A Love Supreme." This haunting recording sounded like one long religious chant and represented his deeply spiritual side. Coltrane died of cancer just three years later at age forty.

AMERICA'S MOST RESPECTED JOURNALIST

Born in Greensboro in 1908, Edward R. Murrow was the most respected journalist in America during the 1940s and 1950s. Murrow joined CBS in 1935. During World War II, he sent live reports from the battlefront in Europe to radio listeners back home.

Back in the United States in 1949, he created the weekly radio program *Hear It Now*, in which he introduced listeners to the most controversial news stories of the day. Murrow quickly became known as one of the nation's boldest radio journalists. In 1951, he created a television version of the program, called *See It Now*. In the next few years, Murrow provided millions of Americans with their first glimpse of many serious social problems, such as the poor treatment of migrant farm workers.

In 1954, CBS broadcast Murrow's most controversial program, an exposé of Senator Joseph McCarthy. McCarthy believed that communists had infiltrated all levels of public life, including the government and the entertainment industry. He called anyone suspected of being a member of—or sympathetic to—the Communist Party to testify before a congressional committee. Witnesses were

MAYA ANGELOU

Celebrated poet, novelist, and civil rights activist Maya Angelou has been a resident of Winston-Salem, where she is a professor at Wake Forest University, since 1981. In much of her writing, Angelou focuses on racial conflict and healing. Her most famous book, *I Know Why the Caged Bird Sings*, describes the violent childhood of an African-American girl. Angelou is committed to reaching out to all types of people through her writing: "You pick yourself up, dust yourself off, and prepare to love somebody. I don't mean sentimentality. I mean the condition of the human spirit, so profound that it encourages us to build bridges."

Like much of Angelou's writing, the following poem, "Still I Rise," describes a person's triumph over suffering and persecution.

Out of the huts of history's shame
I rise
Up from a past that's rooted in pain
I rise
I'm a black ocean, leaping and wide,
Welling and swelling I bear in the tide.
Leaving behind nights of terror and fear
I rise
Into a daybreak that's wondrously clear
I rise
Bringing the gifts that my ancestors gave,
I am the dream and the hope of the slave.
I rise
I rise
I rise.

Edward R. Murrow took the responsibility of his job seriously. "Just because your voice reaches halfway around the world doesn't mean you are wiser than when it reached only to the end of the bar," he once said.

asked about their own activities; they were also asked to provide names of others connected to the party. Many people were arrested because of their connections to communism—or for refusing to testify before the committee. Countless others lost their jobs.

McCarthy became so powerful that most people were afraid to challenge him. But Edward Murrow was never afraid of anyone. He felt that the senator had gone too far, that he was depriving people of the rights to privacy and freedom of speech that were provided by the Constitution. On *Hear It Now*, Murrow presented his viewers with a thorough examination of McCarthy's abusive, sometimes illegal tactics.

"We will not walk in fear, one of another," Murrow proclaimed at the end of the broadcast. "We will not be driven by fear into an age of unreason if we dig deep in our history and doctrine and remember that we are not descended from fearful men, not from men who feared to write, to speak, to associate and to defend causes which were for the moment unpopular." After the program aired, public support for McCarthy's anticommunist investigations began to drop, and the committee hearings were soon stopped.

6 FROM MOUNTAIN TO BEACH

North Carolina is a fascinating mix of dramatic peaks, white beaches, sleepy towns, and thriving cities. Let's take a quick tour of some of them.

THE MOUNTAINS

Western North Carolina's biggest attraction is the Blue Ridge Parkway. This scenic roadway snakes through the mountains from the Virginia state line in the north all the way to the Tennessee border to the east. Cars creep along the parkway at a snail's pace as their passengers take in the breathtaking mountain views that spread out in every direction.

A popular stop is spectacular Grandfather Mountain. The most exciting thing about Grandfather Mountain is the swinging bridge that connects two towering peaks. On clear days, visitors who are brave enough to cross the bridge can gaze straight down into the valley that plunges below their feet. "I've been to Grandfather Mountain at least a dozen times over the years," says a store owner from Boone, "but I still feel the same fear and excitement every time I walk across that old bridge. You look out all around you in every direction, and you feel like you're floating on top of the world. It makes me feel dizzy just thinking about it."

Hidden away in the heart of the Great Smoky Mountains is the

A woman and child cross Grandfather Mountain's swinging bridge over a valley that plunges a mile below.

Cherokee reservation, the largest Indian reservation in the eastern United States. The reservation is the original hiding place of the Cherokee people who escaped capture by federal troops in 1838. A highlight of the reservation is a re-created Cherokee village from the colonial period, known as the Oconaluftee Indian Village. There you can see tiny clay-and-log houses like those in which

Cherokees lived more than 250 years ago. You can also watch young Cherokee men demonstrate traditional skills with blowguns and bows-and-arrows.

ASHEVILLE

Perched on the eastern rim of the Blue Ridge Mountains, Asheville is a rich blend of traditional and modern elements. Over the years, it has been home to several of the state's most prominent citizens,

Oconoluftee Indian Village takes you back to the way Cherokees lived in the eighteenth century. Here, craftspeople demonstrate how masks were made.

including politician Zebulon B. Vance and novelist Thomas Wolfe. Vance was a popular governor and senator in the years following the Civil War. An enormous statue honoring his achievements is located in Pack Square near the heart of downtown. A few blocks away, Wolfe's childhood home has been restored as a museum celebrating his life and work.

More than anything else, Asheville is known for its splendid architecture. Several of Asheville's tall buildings date from the 1920s, when sharp angles and gleaming steel supports were popular. Erected in 1925, the fifteen-story Jackson Building was the city's first skyscraper. It still casts a dark shadow over the people strolling along Pack Square. Across from Pack Square, city hall was designed to resemble a mountain fortress. Completed in 1928, it is made of a colorful blend of marble, brick, and terra-cotta. Its architect, Douglas D. Ellington, reportedly designed the building's eight-sided roof to resemble the traditional headdress worn by Native Americans from the region.

Asheville has long been a popular gathering place for people interested in bluegrass music and mountain folk art. Painters, wood-carvers and instrument makers sell their work in small stores throughout the city. And on most evenings, musicians playing blue-grass and old-time mountain songs perform around the city. In recent years, Asheville has also begun to attract young people involved in more modern music and art. In the city's parks and public plazas, experimental painters, musicians, and performance artists occasionally display their talent alongside traditional musi-cians and craftspeople. "It's really amazing, if you think about it," says a young classical musician who recently moved to the area,

The eight-sided dome on Asheville's city hall is one of the town's most notable landmarks.

"that such a small, seemingly isolated place could have room for so many types of people and so many forms of artistic expression. There's old-time music, performance art, rock and roll, jazz. It's all here in Asheville."

CHARLOTTE

Snuggled beneath the foothills of the Appalachian Mountains, Charlotte is North Carolina's largest city. It is filled with art galleries

THE BILTMORE HOUSE

Outside of Asheville stands one of the state's most impressive landmarks, the lavish Biltmore Estate. Completed in 1895 for George Washington Vanderbilt of the famous shipping and railroad family, the estate took six years to build and was designed to rival the great country manors of Europe.

The largest and most expensive home ever built in the United States, the Biltmore manor has 255 rooms, covering more than four acres of floor space. In all, the mansion features thirty-four bedrooms, forty-three bathrooms, and sixty-five working fireplaces. It also has an indoor bowling alley and swimming pool. The grounds are as impressive as the manor itself, with 125,000 acres of forests and parks and an 8,000-acre garden.

"I think of the Biltmore House as one of North Carolina's finest treasures," says a Durham resident. "It's a fairy tale house of wealth and splendor and pleasure. Everything there is larger than life, from the bookcases to the portraits to the staircases. The first time I saw it decorated for Christmas, I felt like I was in a dream. My eyes could not take in all the beauty."

and museums. One of the South's premier collections, the Mint Museum of Art, was the state's first museum to display classical European and American paintings, and also features one of the nation's finest collections of pottery and porcelain. Another museum, By Hand, focuses on handcrafted work by folk artists and potters from throughout the Southeast. The Tryon Center for Visual Art, located in a beautifully restored church building in the city's historic district, features a spectacular collection of contemporary art.

One of the South's largest and most colorful botanical gardens is located in nearby Belmont. Highlights of the sprawling grounds are the Scroll Garden, which is filled with butterflies and birds, and the Canal Garden, with its amazing tropical flowers.

RALEIGH

In the heart of the Piedmont region is the state capitol of Raleigh. The capitol building occupies two entire tree-covered blocks at the heart of the city's downtown. With its enormous columns and dome, it is widely regarded as one of the nation's outstanding examples of Greek Revival architecture. The governor's mansion sits at the edge of a historic, tree-lined neighborhood of elaborate nineteenth-century homes. U.S. president Franklin Delano Roosevelt once described it as "the most beautiful governor's residence in America."

More than anywhere else in North Carolina, Charlotte feels like a big city.

PLACES TO SEE

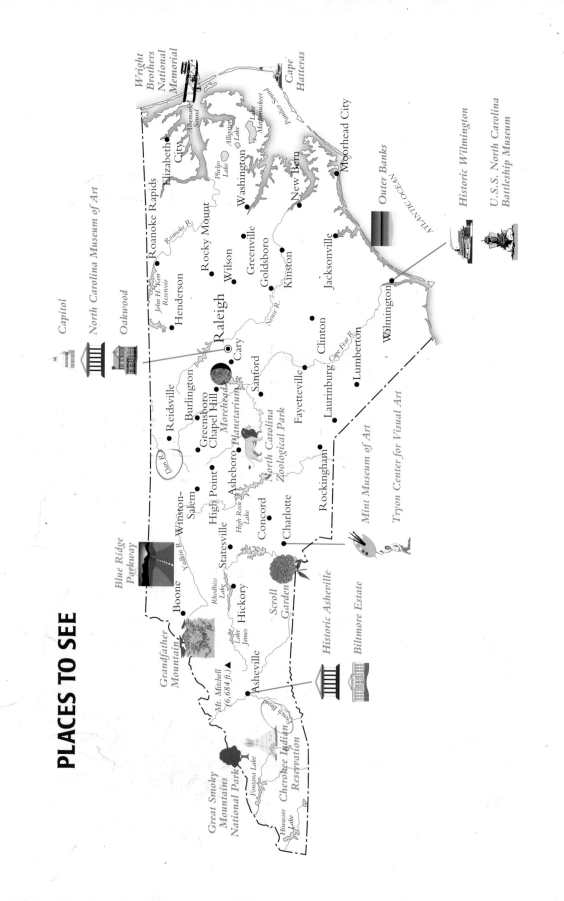

Capitol

North Carolina Museum of Art

Oakwood

Wright Brothers National Memorial

Cape Hatteras

Elizabeth City

Roanoke Rapids

Albemarle Sound

Lake Mattamuskeet

Alligator Lake

Phelps Lake

Moorhead City

Washington

New Bern

Outer Banks

Historic Wilmington

U.S.S. North Carolina Battleship Museum

Rocky Mount

Wilson

Greenville

Goldsboro

Kinston

Jacksonville

ATLANTIC OCEAN

Roanoke R.

John H. Kerr Reservoir

Henderson

Raleigh

Cary

Nease R.

Clinton

Cape Fear R.

Wilmington

Lumberton

Reidsville

Burlington

Greensboro

Chapel Hill

Morehead Planetarium

Sanford

Fayetteville

Laurinburg

Mint Museum of Art

Tryon Center for Visual Art

North Carolina Zoological Park

Dan R.

Asheboro

Rockingham

Blue Ridge Parkway

Winston-Salem

High Point

High Rock Lake

Concord

Charlotte

Yadkin R.

Statesville

Boone

Rhodhiss Lake

Hickory

Scroll Garden

Historic Asheville

Biltmore Estate

Grandfather Mountain

Lake James

Asheville

Mt. Mitchell (6,684 ft.) ▲

French Broad

Great Smoky Mountains National Park

Cherokee Indian Reservation

Fontana Lake

Hiwassee Lake

TEN LARGEST CITIES

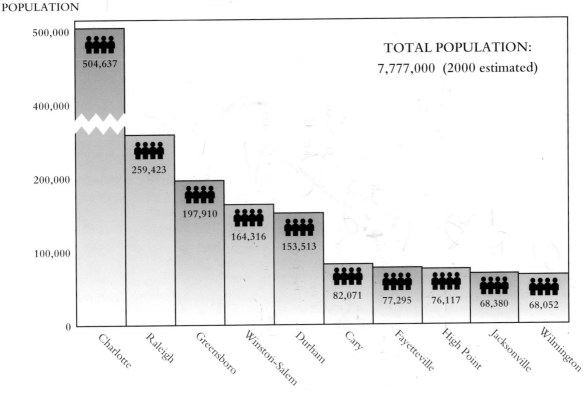

POPULATION

TOTAL POPULATION:
7,777,000 (2000 estimated)

500,000

504,637

400,000

259,423

200,000

197,910

164,316

153,513

100,000

82,071   77,295   76,117   68,380   68,052

0

Charlotte   Raleigh   Greensboro   Winston-Salem   Durham   Cary   Fayetteville   High Point   Jacksonville   Wilmington

Raleigh is known as a city of parks, gardens, and nature trails. The metropolitan area has 150 major parks. Not far from downtown, Pullen Park features a carousel, a miniature train ride, and paddleboats. During the spring and summer, Shelley Lake is filled with sailboats and pedalboats, as runners circle the Greenway trail bordering the water. "There's not a better place in this country to live and raise a family," brags a government employee in Raleigh. "The whole area is covered with dogwoods and pine trees, and in the spring and the summer, the roads and the sidewalks are lined with flowers. And you never have a problem finding a place to play ball with your kids or have a picnic with your family. The whole city feels like it was made for people to live in, and that's something you just don't see that much of these days."

WILMINGTON

Located near the state's southeastern corner, Wilmington is North Carolina's leading seaport and one of its fastest-growing cities. A major part of Wilmington's appeal lies in the preservation of its colorful history. Historic downtown Wilmington features trolleys and vintage riverboats docked in the harbor. With its 230 blocks of restored buildings and landmarks, it is one of the largest historic districts in the nation. Visitors can either tour the area by foot or hitch a ride in a horse-drawn carriage.

Docked on Cape Fear River is another piece of history, the North Carolina Memorial Battleship. Nicknamed the Showboat, the enormous ship was an important part of every major sea battle in the Pacific Ocean during the war.

THE OUTER BANKS

Most of the coastline north of Wilmington is guarded by the narrow string of islands known as the Outer Banks. The islands of the Outer

When the North Carolina *was active during World War II, it was the most powerful battleship in the world.*

Banks are connected to the mainland by a series of towering bridges that sweep up from one shore and down onto the other. Most people who visit the area come to see the snowy white beaches.

North of Wilmington, the jagged beach of Cape Hatteras juts out into the Atlantic Ocean like a giant elbow. Known as the Graveyard of the Atlantic, the cape has been the site of countless boating accidents over the years. Time and time again, boats have ventured too close to the shore and lost control in the powerful waters. In 1870, one of the largest lighthouses on the East Coast was erected at the tip of the cape to warn ships approaching the shore. Today, this magnificent brick structure is painted in stripes of black and white and rises 180 feet above the shore.

Farther north on the Outer Banks is the hilly stretch of beach known as Nags Head. Visitors to the area enjoy climbing to the top of the enormous dunes, which provide spectacular views of the blue, white-capped water of the Atlantic.

A few miles north are the beaches of Kitty Hawk and Kill Devil Hills. A ninety-one-foot monument at the top of Big Kill Devil Hill marks the site where the Wright brothers made the world's first motorized flight in 1903. You can also visit replicas of the hangar and workshop where the Wright brothers built and repaired their airplanes. Today, visitors fly kites—instead of airplanes—in the powerful winds that blow across the beach.

The 208-foot-tall Cape Hatteras Lighthouse has guarded the shore since 1870, but in 1999 it was moved 2,900 feet inland to keep it from tipping over as the beach crumbled beneath it.

"There's so much to see in North Carolina," says a recent visitor to Kill Devil Hills. "There's so much history and so much beauty right here side by side. When I was growing up, folks used to argue about which was the best—the mountains or the ocean. But if

The sand dunes along the Outer Banks have become a popular spot for hang gliding.

you're honest with yourself, there's really no way you can make a choice. You just have to see them both—and everything that's in between. That's the only way you can really get to know North Carolina."

THE FLAG: The right-hand side of the state flag is composed of a red bar above a white bar. On the left is a blue vertical stripe with a white star and the letters N and C in the center. Above the star is a scroll bearing the date May 20, 1775, the day Mecklenburg County is said to have declared independence from Britain. Below it is a scroll bearing the date April 12, 1776, when North Carolina agreed that delegates to the Continental Congress should vote for American independence.

THE SEAL: The state seal was adopted in 1971. On the left, a figure representing liberty holds a scroll bearing the word Constitution. On the right, a seated figure represents plenty. Below them is the state motto in Latin, Esse quam videri. The dates that appear on the flag also appear on the state seal.

STATE SURVEY

Statehood: November 21, 1789

Origin of Name: The region was named *Carolana*, which means "land of Charles" in Latin, after King Charles I of England.

Nickname: Tar Heel State

Capital: Raleigh

Motto: To Be, Rather Than to Seem

Bird: Cardinal

Flower: Dogwood

Tree: Longleaf pine

Fish: Channel bass

Cardinal

Dogwood

THE OLD NORTH STATE

"The Old North State" was adopted as the official song of North Carolina in 1927.

Insect: Honeybee

Precious Stone: Emerald

Reptile: Eastern box turtle

Rock: Granite

Shell: Scotch bonnet

GEOGRAPHY

Highest Point: 6,684 feet above sea level, at Mount Mitchell

Lowest Point: sea level along the coast

Area: 52,672 square miles

Greatest Distance, North to South: 188 miles

Greatest Distance, East to West: 499 miles

Bordering States: Virginia to the north, Tennessee to the west, South Carolina and Georgia to the south

Hottest Recorded Temperature: 110°F at Fayetteville on August 21, 1983

Coldest Recorded Temperature: -34°F at Mount Mitchell on January 21, 1985

Average Annual Precipitation: 50 inches

Major Rivers: Cape Fear, Catawba, Little Tennessee, Nantahala, Neuse, Roanoke, Tar, Yadkin

Major Lakes: Fontana, High Rock, Mattamuskeet, New, Norman, Phelps

Trees: cedar, cypress, gum, hickory, loblolly pine, maple, oak, pine, tulip tree

Wild Plants: azalea, camellia, dogwood, orchid, pitcher plant, redbud, rhododendron, sundew

Animals: beaver, black bear, dolphin, fox, otter, rabbit, raccoon, skunk, white-tailed deer

Dolphin

Birds: Carolina wren, duck, goose, mockingbird, mourning dove, partridge, swan, woodcock

Fish: bass, bluegill, crappie, flounder, marlin, menhaden, sailfish, sturgeon, sunfish, trout

Leatherback sea turtle

Endangered Animals: Appalachian elktoe, Cape Fear shiner, Carolina heelsplitter, Carolina northern flying squirrel, dwarf wedgemussel, eastern puma, finback whale, humpback whale, Indiana bat, Kemp's ridley sea turtle, leatherback sea turtle, littlewing pearlymussel, red wolf, red-cockaded woodpecker, right whale, roseate tern, Saint Francis' satyr butterfly, shortnose sturgeon, sperm whale, spruce-fir moss spider, Tar River spinymussel, Virginia big-eared bat, West Indian manatee

Endangered Plants: American chaffseed, bunched arrowhead, Canby's dropwort, Cooley's meadowrue, green pitcher-plant, harperella, Michaux's sumac, mountain sweet pitcher-plant, pondberry, Roan Mountain bluet, rock gnome lichen, rough-leaved loosestrife, Schweinitz's sunflower, small-anthered bittercress, smooth coneflower, spreading avens, white irisette

TIMELINE

North Carolina History

1400s Cherokee, Hatteras, Catawba, Chowanoc, Tuscarora, and other Indians live in what is now North Carolina

1524 Giovanni da Verrazano becomes the first European to explore the North Carolina coast

1540 Spaniard Hernando de Soto becomes the first white man to cross North Carolina's southwestern mountains

1585 The first English colony in what is now the United States is established at Roanoke Island

1587 Virginia Dare of Roanoke Island becomes the first English child born in America

1650 North Carolina's first permanent white settlement is established near Albemarle Sound

1705 Bath, North Carolina's first town, is incorporated; North Carolina's first school opens near Elizabeth City

1711 Tuscarora Indians attack white settlements, killing hundreds of people and marking the beginning of the Tuscarora War

1712 North Carolina and South Carolina become separate colonies

1751 The *North Carolina Gazette*, the region's first newspaper, begins publication

1775–1783 The American Revolution

1789 North Carolina becomes the 12th state

1795 The University of North Carolina becomes the first public university to begin holding classes

1861 The Civil War begins; North Carolina secedes from the Union

1871 North Carolinian William W. Holden becomes the nation's first governor to be impeached

1903 Wilbur and Orville Wright make the world's first successful motorized airplane flight at Kill Devil Hills

1917 The United States enters World War I

1935 Construction begins on the Blue Ridge Parkway, a scenic route linking national parks in Virginia and North Carolina

1941–1945 Nearly 370,000 North Carolinians serve in the armed forces during World War I

1959 North Carolina Research Triangle Park, which is run by three universities to serve industry, opens. It brings prosperity to Durham, Raleigh, and Chapel Hill

1960 Four black students start the sit-in movement at a lunch counter in Greensboro, in protest of being refused service

1971 The state's third and present constitution goes into effect

1972 Jesse Helms becomes the first Republican elected to the U.S. Senate from North Carolina since 1895

1989 Hurricane Hugo strikes North Carolina, devastating the state as far inland as Charlotte

1994 The Raleigh-Durham area is ranked best place to live in the United States by *Money* magazine

1996 Hurricane Fran pounds North Carolina, causing $1 billion in damage

ECONOMY

Agricultural Products: apples, blueberries, catfish, chickens, corn, hogs, milk, peaches, peanuts, soybeans, strawberries, sweet potatoes, tobacco, turkeys

Blueberries

Manufactured Products: carpeting, chemicals, cigarettes, cloth, computers, construction equipment, food products, furniture, hosiery, telephone equipment, yarn

Natural Resources: crushed stone, feldspar, fish, sand and gravel, shellfish

Business and Trade: banking, insurance, real estate, research, tourism, wholesale and retail trade

CALENDAR OF CELEBRATIONS

North Carolina Azalea Festival Each spring when North Carolina's azaleas burst into bloom, Wilmington celebrates with a long weekend of garden tours, concerts, and a grand parade.

Ham and Yam Festival More yams are grown in Johnston County than any other county in the United States. In April, Smithfield serves them up in style with another North Carolina specialty, home-cured country ham.

Shad Festival Every April, Grifton throws a party in honor of the shad, a small, bony fish that swims in a creek at the edge of town.

North Carolina Blackbeard Festival The most notorious sailor ever to torment the eastern seaboard takes center stage at this May celebration in Morehead City. Special events include a re-created pirate battle, a treasure hunt, and a Blackbeard look-alike contest.

Fossil Festival Visitors to Aurora get a free guided tour of nearby fossil beds during this May event. Guests can dig for their own fossils or examine those on display in town, along with a wide array of minerals.

Highland Games and Gathering of the Clans Grandfather Mountain hosts the country's largest Scottish games in July with traditional dancing and piping, sheepdog-herding demonstrations, and athletic contests.

Highland Games and Gathering of the Clans

Mountain Dance and Folk Festival The best musicians and dancers of the Appalachians perform at this August festival in Asheville.

Benson Mule Days Each September you'll see Benson's most stubborn animals perform all kinds of amazing feats, from leaping tall fences to pulling massive loads. The best of the bunch leads a parade of 2,000 mules and horses through the center of town.

Cherokee Indian Fair Each October Native Americans celebrate their heritage during a five-day festival in Cherokee. Activities include stickball games, archery and blowgun contests, and traditional dancing.

John Blue Cotton Festival Laurinburg takes a step back in time the second weekend in October with exhibits including a mule-driven cotton gin and a grist mill. Don't miss the old-fashioned Sunday church service.

Woolly Worm Festival Legend has it you can tell whether a hard winter is coming by the stripes on the woolly worm, a fuzzy black and reddish brown caterpillar. But since each caterpillar is different, forecasts aren't always consistent. Every fall Banner Elk holds a woolly worm race to see which caterpillar should be the final authority.

Core Sound Decoy Festival The art of carving wooden duck decoys has a long history in coastal North Carolina. December brings hundreds of artists and collectors to Harkers Island, where locals celebrate the craft with carving competitions, a loon-calling contest, and a fair featuring new and antique decoys.

STATE STARS

David Brinkley (1920–) is a prominent television journalist and commentator. In the 1960s, Brinkley became a household name as co-anchor, with Chet Huntley, of television's *Huntley-Brinkley Report*. He later hosted his own news show, *This Week with David Brinkley*. Brinkley, who was born in Wilmington, has won ten Emmy Awards and two Peabodys for outstanding television journalism.

David Brinkley

John Coltrane (1926–1967), one of the world's greatest saxophonists, was born in Hamlet. As a young man, Coltrane played sax in the style of the legendary Charlie Parker, but by the late 1950s he had developed a way of playing all his own, featuring intense, elaborate solos and rapid improvisation. Brilliant on both alto and tenor sax, Coltrane also gave the soprano sax its first major role in jazz. His most famous recordings include *A Love Supreme* and *My Favorite Things*.

Cecil B. DeMille (1881–1959) was an influential film director and producer. In 1913, DeMille helped make Hollywood's first feature-length movie, *The Squaw Man*. DeMille later directed such sweeping epics as *The Greatest Show on Earth*, for which he won an Academy Award, and the hugely popular *The Ten Commandments*. DeMille spent most of his childhood in Washington.

Cecil B. DeMille

Elizabeth Dole (1936–   ), a leading Republican politician, has held posts under six different presidents, including serving as secretary of labor under Ronald Reagan and secretary of transportation under George Bush. In 1991, Dole became president of the American Red Cross, and in 2000 she campaigned for the Republican presidential nomination. Dole was born in Salisbury.

James Buchanan Duke (1856–1925) of Durham turned his family's tobacco processing business into one of the country's biggest industries. Duke used new technology and advertising to make cigarette manufacturing profitable, then bought up competitors to create a vast tobacco empire. When he died he left a trust fund to Durham's Trinity College, now known as Duke University.

Roberta Flack

Roberta Flack (1939–   ), a church organist's daughter from Black Mountain, hit the top of the pop charts in 1972 with her smooth rendition of the song "The First Time Ever I Saw Your Face." Flack's velvety voice and elegant style on ballads like "Killing Me Softly with His Song" and "Set the Night to Music" made a huge impact on popular music in the 1970s and 1980s.

Ava Gardner (1922–1990) was a sultry, glamorous film actress. Born near Smithfield, Gardner was discovered by Hollywood after her brother-in-law, a photographer, displayed pictures of her in the window of his New York studio. She went on to play the romantic lead in such classic films as *Show Boat*, *One Touch of Venus*, and *On the Beach*.

Richard Gatling (1818–1903) invented the Gatling gun, one of the first machine guns to be effective in war. During his childhood in Hertford

County, Gatling helped his father design a machine for sowing cotton. He grew up to develop a series of mechanical devices, including the gun that bears his name. The Gatling gun, which could fire close to 300 rounds a minute, was heavily used by the U.S. Army in the late 19th century.

Billy Graham (1918–   ), a native of Charlotte, is one of America's most famous preachers and a leading spokesman for conservative Christianity. Graham went on his first major preaching tour of the United States and Europe in 1949. He has since traveled the globe many times, captivating listeners with his fiery, eloquent sermons.

Billy Graham

Andy Griffith (1926–   ), who grew up in Mount Airy, was the longtime star of *The Andy Griffith Show*, a 1960s television show about life in the fictional North Carolina town of Mayberry. He later played a cool-headed lawyer in the television series *Matlock*.

Mia Hamm (1972–   ), who makes her home in Chapel Hill, is one of the most talented female soccer players in the world. In 1987, at age 15, Hamm became the youngest person ever to join the U.S. national soccer team. She later led North Carolina's Tar Heels to four national championships and became the top scorer in NCAA women's soccer history. Hamm's fast and

Mia Hamm

accurate playing style helped the U.S. national team win the Women's World Cup in 1991 and 1999.

Jesse Helms (1921–) has been a U.S. senator from North Carolina since 1973. Born in Monroe, Helms worked as a journalist and a television executive in Raleigh before entering politics. Known for his outspoken conservatism on social issues, in 1995 he became chairman of the influential Senate Foreign Relations Committee.

O. Henry (1862–1910) is the pen name of William Sydney Porter, a short story writer famous for his surprise endings. Although he turned to writing late in life, this Greensboro native became one of the most popular writers of his generation, publishing hundreds of short stories during his career. Today, his contribution to the short story is remembered with the O. Henry Memorial Awards, which are given each year to the best American short stories.

Andrew Johnson (1808–1875), a native of Raleigh, was the 17th president of the United States. Johnson entered politics after moving to Tennessee, where he became famous for his powerful speeches in defense of the working class. He was elected vice president shortly before President Abraham Lincoln was assassinated in 1865. As Lincoln's successor, Johnson quickly became unpopular with northern politicians who thought he was too forgiving toward the South. In 1868, he became the first president to be impeached, which means the U.S. House voted that the Senate should hold a trial to decide whether he should be removed from office. The Senate, however, voted not to remove him.

Michael Jordan (1963–   ) is widely regarded as the greatest basketball player of all time. Born in Brooklyn, New York, and raised in Wilmington, he played basketball for the University of North Carolina for three years before joining the Chicago Bulls. During his 12-year professional career, he led the Bulls to six championships, and his charismatic personality and spectacular shooting made basketball popular worldwide.

Charles Kuralt (1934–1997) was an award-winning journalist whose reports on small town America charmed television audiences for more than 30 years. He won three Peabody Awards and ten Emmys for his programs *On the Road with Charles Kuralt* and *Sunday Morning*. Kuralt was born in Wilmington.

Sugar Ray Leonard (1956–   ), one of the most talented boxers of his generation, won five world titles, beating his opponents in the welterweight, super welterweight, and middleweight classes. Leonard won the gold

Sugar Ray Leonard

medal in the light welterweight division in the 1976 Olympics. He is a native of Wilmington.

Dolley Madison (1768–1849) was one of the most celebrated first ladies in U.S. history. Born in Guilford County, she became active in Washington, D.C., society after marrying congressman James Madison in 1794. During Madison's presidency from 1809 to 1817, she charmed the nation's capital with her Wednesday receptions, in which politicians, diplomats, and the public came together for an evening of socializing that eased political tensions.

Dolley Madison

John Merrick (1859–1919), a successful businessman, was born into slavery in Clinton and was brought up without formal schooling. After years of hard work in construction and shoeshining, he opened a barber shop in Durham and soon became a leader in the black business community. In 1898 he helped found the North Carolina Mutual and Provident Insurance Company in Durham, soon to become the nation's largest African-American-owned business.

Thelonius Monk (1917–1982) was a jazz pianist who, along with saxophonist Charlie Parker and trumpeter Dizzy Gillespie, helped create the fast, complex bebop style. Marked by uneven rhythms and strange sounds, Monk's music was so unusual that during his early years, jazz

Thelonius Monk

lovers sometimes thought he couldn't play well. It wasn't until the mid-1950s that he gained recognition as a groundbreaking pianist and composer. Today, his haunting melodies, notably "'Round Midnight," "Evidence," and "Misterioso," are among the most admired in jazz. Monk was born in Rocky Mount.

Edward R. Murrow (1908–1965) was a highly respected radio and television journalist. A Greensboro native, Murrow joined the CBS news team in 1935 and first gained acclaim for his on-the-scenes reporting during World War II. Afer the war he developed the radio program *Hear It Now*, and later the television program *See It Now*, both of which dealt with controversial issues. In 1954 Murrow caused a sensation on his show when he took on Senator Joseph McCarthy's anti-communist crusade.

Richard Petty (1937–   ) is one of the greatest stock car drivers in racing history. Born in Randleman, Petty caught the racing bug from his father, stock car Hall of Famer Lee Petty. Richard eventually became his sport's all-time champion, with seven driver titles and 200 career wins.

Richard Petty

James K. Polk (1795–1849), the 11th president of the United States, believed the nation was destined to expand west to the Pacific Ocean. His belief came true in 1848 during his presidency, when the United States aquired California and much of the Southwest at the end of the Mexican War. Polk was born in Mecklenburg County.

James K. Polk

Nina Simone (1933–   ) is a singer, songwriter, and pianist from Tryon. Simone recorded her first hit, the George Gershwin song "I Loves You Porgy," in the late 1950s. Since then she has used her strange, deep voice to sing everything from gospel and jazz to blues and folk.

Doc Watson (1923–   ) is a blues musician known for his down-home brilliance on the accoustic guitar. Born in Stoney Fork and raised in Deep Gap, Arthel "Doc" Watson lost his vision before he was one year old. After learning guitar as a teenager, he devoted himself to playing the music he grew up with, from country hits to old-time fiddle tunes. Watson earned widespread acclaim after the release of his album *Doc Watson* in 1964. Since then he has been honored with five Grammy Awards and a National Medal of the Arts.

Thomas Wolfe (1900–1938) is best known for four novels that paint a vivid portrait American life in the early 20th century. Wolfe's *Look Homeward, Angel*, *Of Time and the River*, *The Web and the Rock*, and *You Can't Go Home Again* are set against the backdrop of his native North Carolina. Wolfe was born in Asheville.

TOUR THE STATE

Ocracoke Island This long strip of land about 30 miles offshore boasts quiet towns and beautiful sandy beaches. The pirate Blackbeard once hid out in the rocks on its western shore.

Duke Homestead and Tobacco Museum (Durham) Historic displays tell the story of the tobacco industry at the home of American Tobacco Company founder Washington Duke.

Cherokee Indian Reservation (Cherokee) Native American history and traditions come to life at the Museum of the Cherokee Indian. During the summer, tribe members demonstrate traditional crafts at Okconaluftee Indian Village, built to look like a Cherokee town of the 1700s.

Grandfather Mountain (Linville) Shaped like the face of an old man, this rocky peak features a swinging bridge a mile high.

Battleship *North Carolina* Memorial (Wilmington) One of America's most famous naval ships is docked on the Cape Fear River in Wilmington. The *North Carolina* fought in every major battle in the Pacific during World War II.

Chimney Rock (Chimney Rock) A trip to the top of this dramatic rock formation in Rutherford County guarantees dazzling views of the Blue Ridge Mountains.

Roanoke Island The first two English settlements in the United States were established here in 1585 and 1587. The second mysteriously disappeared. In Manteo, an outdoor musical drama called *The Last Colony* vividly tells the tale.

Jockey's Ridge State Park (Nags Head) Giant dunes make this seaside park look like the Sahara Desert, with its mountains of shifting sands. Strong winds make it a popular spot for hang gliding.

Wright Brothers National Memorial (Kill Devil Hills) A 60-foot granite monument marks the spot where Orville and Wilbur Wright took flight for the first time. Inside the visitors center is a life-sized model of their original plane.

Wright Brothers National Memorial

Old Salem (Winston-Salem) The colonial era is beautifully preserved in this restored village, founded in 1766.

Croatan National Forest (New Bern) The lakes and bogs of this 157,000-acre woods are crowded with insect-eating plants like the sundew, the pitcher plant, and the Venus flytrap.

Biltmore Estate (Asheville) Millionaire George Vanderbilt once entertained guests here in his 255-room chateau. Today, this largest home in America and its formal gardens are open for public tours.

Morehead Planetarium (Chapel Hill) Stars and planets move across a giant dome at this planetarium, where astronauts once practiced navigating by the stars.

Nantahala Gorge (Bryson City) The name of this narrow canyon in the mountains means "Land of the Noonday Sun." The gorge is so deep and narrow that the sun only peeps in around noon.

North Carolina Museum of Art (Raleigh) This renowned art museum displays a wide array of American and European art.

Great Smoky Mountains National Park (Cherokee) About 500 black bears thrive in the country's most popular national park, which straddles the border of North Carolina and Tennessee.

Cape Hatteras Lighthouse (Buxton) Built in 1870, this black-and-white-striped landmark was moved 2,900 feet inland in 1999 to save it from being washed away. It guards Cape Hatteras, which has such treacherous waters it is known as the Graveyard of the Atlantic.

Blue Ridge Parkway (Asheville) America's best-loved scenic drive wanders along the top of the Blue Ridge Mountains, with breathtaking views along the way.

North Carolina Zoological Park (Asheboro) Animals from across North America and Africa can be seen at one of the nation's largest zoos.

Bentonville Battleground State Historic Site North Carolina's last major

Civil War battle was fought near Bentonville. Visitors can tour the farm-house that served as a field hospital during the fighting.

Reed Gold Mine State Historic Site (Stanfield) America's first gold rush was launched by a 12-year-old boy named Conrad Reed in Cabarrus County. You can try your own luck near the spot where his family grew rich panning 115 pounds of gold.

Tobacco Farm Life Museum (Kenly) This restored farmstead and museum offers a glimpse of farm life from the late 19th century through the 1950s.

FUN FACTS

At 411 feet tall, Whitewater Falls in Transylvania County is the highest waterfall on the East Coast.

Baseball legend Babe Ruth hit his first professional home run in Fayetteville on March 7, 1914.

America's smallest town is Dellview, North Carolina. In 1990 it had a population of 10.

FIND OUT MORE

If you want to find out more about North Carolina, check your local library or bookstore for these titles.

GENERAL STATE BOOKS

Hintz, Martin, and Stephen Hintz. *North Carolina*. New York: Children's Press, 1998.

Schulz, Andrea. *North Carolina*. Minneapolis: Lerner, 1998.

SPECIAL INTEREST BOOKS

Beatty, Patricia. *Who Comes with Cannons?* New York: Morrow, 1992.

Haley, Gail E. *Mountain Jack Tales*. New York: Dutton, 1992.

Jordan, Michael. *For the Love of the Game: My Story*. New York: Crown Publishers, 1998.

Lyons, Mary E. *Letters from a Slave Girl: The Story of Harriet Jacobs*. New York: Aladdin, 1996.

Selfridge, John. *John Coltrane: A Sound Supreme*. New York: Franklin Watts, 1999.

Whedbee, Charles Harry. *Black Beard's Cup and Stories of the Outer Banks.* Winston-Salem, NC: John F. Blair Publishers, 1989.

RECORDINGS

Coltrane, John. *A Love Supreme.* Impulse, 1965.

Flatt and Scruggs. *The Complete Mercury Sessions.* Mercury, 1992.

Simone, Nina. *The Essential Nina Simone.* RCA, 1993.

Watson, Doc. *The Essential Doc Watson.* Vanguard, 1987.

WEBSITES

www.50states.com/ncarolin.htm This provides a long list of links on North Carolina history, government, geography, and symbols, including fast facts about the state and brief biographies of famous North Carolinians.

statelibrary.dcr.state.nc.us/ The official resource of the North Carolina state library, this includes a thorough introduction to government, history, geography, and famous people in the state.

www.state.nc.us/ The official state website includes detailed information on North Carolina government, with links to information resources for children.

INDEX

Page numbers for illustrations are in boldface.